Probable Sino-Russia Military Pact

Implications for India

Commodore **SL Deshmukh**, NM (Retd.)

KNOWLEDGE WORLD

KW Publishers Pvt Ltd
New Delhi

Chennai Centre for China Studies

The Chennai Centre for China Studies (C3S), registered under the Tamil Nadu Societies Registration Act 1975 (83/2008 dated 4th April 2008), is a non-profit public policy think tank with the following objectives.

- Carry out in-depth studies of developments relating to China with priority to issues of interest to India such as
    1. Geopolitical, economic and strategic dynamics of India-China relations.
    2. China's internal dynamics.
    3. The Sino-Indian border issue.
    4. China's relations with South Asian countries.
    5. Prospects of Sino-Indian economic and trade relations.
    6. Future evolution of China's politics and its impact on India and the world.
    7. China - India - ASEAN relations.
    8. China's emerging role in SAARC.
    9. Growing importance of South India for Chinese interaction and economic investment.
    10. India - China - Southeast Asia cultural links.
- Suggest viable solutions/policy alternatives on the basis of studies to the strategic planners and decision makers in India, on issues of bilateral, regional and global importance.
- Create public opinion, particularly in South India, on the implications arising out of China's emergence as a leading global power.
- Provide a forum for dialogue with China scholars in India and abroad and give space for expression of alternate opinions on China-related topics.
- Provide a sound data base for research on China with special attention to tapping information available in Chinese language material, so as to benefit scholars, media and think tanks in India as well as rest of the world.
- Address the requirements of the business community in India, particularly informing them about the nature of emerging business opportunities and problems while dealing with China.
- Liaise with think tanks specialising on China, both in India and abroad, with the objective of exchanging views.
- Organise lecture discussions and seminars on topics of current interest.
- Interact with institutions of higher learning in South India to create awareness about developments in China.
- Bring out publications relating to China - books, edited volumes, monographs and occasional papers.

website: www.c3sindia.org

ISBN 978-93-91490-28-7 Paperback

Published in India by Kalpana Shukla

KNOWLEDGE WORLD

KW Publishers Pvt Ltd
4676/21, First Floor, Ansari Road
Daryaganj, New Delhi 110002
Phone: +91 11 43528107
Marketing: kw@kwpub.in
Editorial: production@kwpub.in
Website: www.kwpub.in

Contents

Foreword

First and foremost, must complement my decades old naval colleague Commodore Srikant Deshmukh for taking up a topic of great relevance to policymakers, strategists and academia. With his vast experience in handling projects and having held key appointments both in the Government and private sector, Srikant has taken to writing like fish takes to water and has brought to fore his analytical skills in this monograph which is a delight to read.

The cold war period witnessed a great degree of convergence between the Soviet Union and India. India continues to enjoy very healthy military, strategic and political relations with Russia even after the breaking up of the Soviet Union in 1989. However, the ascendency of China and its economic engagements with the rest of the world have changed the equations in China's favour. With a surging economy of nearly US$ 14 trillion, second only to the USA, China has used its money power to change the narrative of global equations. While questions on whether the spread of COVID was an abetted act are still being examined, the COVID which originated in China has affected all countries around the world. China which was alleged to be behind the spread of the virus willy-nilly appears to have gained from the aftermath of COVID which spread like wildfire changing international relations. COVID or no COVID, Russia and China relations, even if one would like to term it as "convenient relations" are flourishing. This despite the differences on many issues which requires India to take stock of the emerging nature of such relations and the possible impact on its own trajectory post-COVID.

Barring a few rich nations, most countries have come under the spell of China which has used its money power to build constituencies and obtain leverages in countries both far and near. Russia is no exception as it also plans to rebuild its economy. India which is facing a Trans Himalayan aggression has stood up to China militarily and politically impacting the global ambitions of China. Both China and India continue to obtain military hardware and expertise from Russia. Most of the Chinese military forces are built around Russian technology along with key technology that is obtained by IPR violations and espionage. India has been traditionally a major importer of arms for its military from Russia though in the last decade or so, there has been greater diversification of imports from other sources.

It is in this context that this study by Srikant is of great relevance as it examines all the related areas of China Russia military pact. The author is to be complimented for the scholarship demonstrated in constructing a logical narrative with a critical examination of the selected issues under five chapters. There is a refreshing change in the way the topic has been handled by presenting all facts both for and against and then carrying out a dispassionate analysis based on the inferences at the end of each chapter. The chapter on implications for India and the way ahead are of great relevance to the policymakers and need to be factored in the matrix of our future transactions both with Russia and China.

Overall, this a great first effort by Srikant to grasp the nuances of an emerging relationship between Russia and China even if it is due to mutual compulsions and necessity. I would like to wish Srikant all the best in similar efforts in future to contribute to a larger audience both in India and abroad.

Jai Hind

Commodore **RS Vasan** IN Retd.
Director C3S and Regional Director NMF TN

Acknowledgements

The author would like to acknowledge the guidance and constant motivation received from Commodore RS Vasan. My thanks are due to him for Foreword to this monograph. The author would also, like to put his thanks on records for nuanced discussions with Dr R Srinivasan and valuable support from Ms Sujata Deshmukh.

Abstract

Franklin D Roosevelt had said: "In politics, nothing happens by accident. If it happens, you can bet it was planned that way." An analysis of classic Sino-Russia relationship would prove the point.

There is talk now about the "China-Russia" Military Pact. Given the status of current Indo-China relations and Russia's dilemma about its bilateral relations with India and China, the probable "Sino-Russia Military Pact" should be a matter of concern for India, considering its unavoidable impact.

The issues related to Indo-Sino-Russian relations, in their own sphere, are quite complex. Keeping that complexity in mind, the impact of India's multi-dimensional relationship with other countries—especially the USA and the formation of QUAD (USA-Australia-Japan-India) would also be an important factor for consideration. Thus, a broad level analysis of all the aspects mentioned above would be essential to arrive at a conclusion, having the semblance of reality.

The monograph will try to analyse Sino-Russia Military Strategies, their common thread, India's multipronged relationships with other countries, Implications of Sino-Russia pact on India and evaluate measures India could take to safeguard its own national interests.

Keywords: India, Russia, China, Military pact, Impact, USA, South China Sea

Introduction

To quote William Clay "This is quite a game, politics. There are no permanent enemies, and no permanent friends, only permanent interests. This has been reflected in Sino-Russia relations, which have generally followed a classic 'Blow hot-Blow Cold' pattern.

There is a talk now about the 'China-Russia' Military Pact. Given the fact that currently, Indo-China relations are at a lower ebb and Russia-India's all-weather friend-becoming increasingly perturbed with India's growing closeness to the USA; the probable Sino-Russia Military Pact would certainly have an impact on India in Socio-political-economic-strategic-military spheres.

The monograph will try to analyse various implications of the 'China-Russia Military Pact' on India and evaluate possible measures India could take to safeguard its own national interests. It may be noted that the analytical thread would need to weave through Military Strategies of China-Russia, their interlinking, bilateral Sino-India and Sino-Russia relations, their linkage with Indo-US relations, to arrive at a holistic picture.

For clarity the monograph would be covered in various Chapters covering China and Russia Military Strategies and the common thread between them which would be relevant to the topic, examining factors enhancing the probability of Sino-Russia Military Pact and its implication for India, explore cogent measure to mitigate the impact on India and make some viable recommendations for implementation.

1. China and Russia Military Strategies and Common Thread

Military Strategy has been defined by Encyclopaedia Britannica as "Strategy, in warfare, the science or art of employing all the military, economic, political, and other resources of a country to achieve the objects of war." Thus every country formulates its own Military Strategy based on its strategic national interests. To quote Ex-President of US Richard M Nixon "*A riot is a spontaneous outburst. A war is subject to advance planning*". This would explain the importance of a well-defined Military Strategy.

China's Military Strategy

The importance of studying China's Military Strategy till now has been given secondary importance by India. In the current dynamic scenario, thorough knowledge of China's current Military Strategy would be imperative for India.

Image Courtesy Wikimedia

China has displayed its clear understanding of the depth of the Sun Tzu's words "Strategy without tactics is the slowest route to victory. Tactics without strategy is the noise before defeat", as well as of the fact that—to be powerful, it would need to be both economically and militarily strong. China has consistently built its economic and military prowess to fulfil its ambition of becoming the world's Super Power. All its strategies, including the military strategy and maneuverers, have always been directed towards that goal.

The State Council Information Office of the People's Republic of China (SCI-PRC 2015) has pointed out that "China's national strategic goal has been to complete the building of a moderately prosperous society in all respects by 2021, when the CPC celebrates its centenary; and the building of a modern socialist country that is prosperous, strong, democratic, culturally advanced and harmonious by 2049, when the People's Republic of China (PRC) marks its centenary. To achieve the specified goals, building economically and militarily strong China has been an imperative." The release of China's Military Strategy-2019 was a major step in that direction. Since 2015, China has steadfastly focused on the above-stated goal and its Military Strategy, announced in July 2019, has followed the trend.

A major and important event related to the release of the Chinese official strategic document (a White Paper): *China's National Defence in the New Era*, on July 24, 2019 (both in Chinese and English), was almost missed by the world in the conundrum of Iran-Gulf imbroglio and Brexit drama.

US Centric Aspects of the 2019 White Paper

In relation to this White Paper Cordesman (Cordesman 2019) has said "Unlike China's previous defence white paper—the one which came out in 2015 and was blandly reassuring to the point of being vacuous—the new White Paper picks up the gauntlet thrown by the US in terms of its 2017 *National Security Strategy* and 2018 *National Defence Strategy*. Both of these documents effectively made China the key objective in strengthening US military forces and singled it out as America's primary strategic competitor."

He further observed that 'White Paper' titled *China's National Defence in the New Era* (July 24, 2019 has been in a clear response to the massive shift in US strategy from a focus on counterterrorism and extremism to competition and possible conflict with China and Russia. The white paper flags the fact that America and China are now competing superpowers, and that China's growing military forces are developing to the point where they will be able to challenge the United States." More than that, the detailed contents of the White Paper are in direct response to the official US reports on *Chinese Military Power* issued by the Office of the Secretary of Defence and by the Defence Intelligence Agency.

The White Paper summarises the overall character of the United States defence efforts. It declares that the region has become a focus of major country competition, bringing uncertainties to regional security. The paper further states that the US has been strengthening its Asia-Pacific military alliances and reinforcing military deployment and intervention, adding complexity to regional security. It opined that the US deployment of the Terminal High Altitude Area Defence

(THAAD) system in the Republic of Korea (ROK) has severely undermined the regional strategic balance and the strategic security interests of regional countries.

The White Paper describes Taiwan, Tibetan, and Turkistan separatists as threats, the dangers of disputes over territory, and again highlights the US by noting that, "Countries from outside the region conduct frequent close-in reconnaissance on China by air and sea and illegally enter China's territorial waters and the waters and airspace near China's islands and reefs, undermining China's national security."

The July 2019 China's defence White Paper goes on to address virtually every major aspect of Chinese military activity and development as peaceful. For example, it deals with the South China Sea issue by stating that "China's armed forces defend important waters, islands and reefs in the East China Sea, the South China Sea and the Yellow Sea, acquire full situation awareness of adjacent waters, conduct joint rights protection and law enforcement operations, properly handle maritime and air situations, and resolutely respond to security threats, infringements and provocations on the sea.

Cordesman (2019) opined that "One does not have to read between the lines of the White Paper to see that it clearly identifies China as a major strategic competitor to the United States. The text seems to be very careful; however, to limit the level of this competition, and reflects China's understanding of the risks involved".

Seen from that perspective, the Chinese White Paper—like the two recent US national strategy documents cited at the beginning—gives a clear warning of growing strategic rivalry between an existing and emerging superpower that has already become stronger than Russia in virtually every respect, other than its number of nuclear weapons. This warning would certainly shape the future of both China and the US, for decades to come.

Military and Security Cooperation

China's White Paper (July 2019) states that "Pursuing a security concept featuring common, comprehensive, cooperative and sustainable security, China's armed forces will continue to develop military-to-military relations that are non-aligned, non-confrontational and not directed against any third party. They will strive to establish fair and effective collective security mechanisms and military confidence-building measures (CBMs), expand military and security cooperation, and create a security environment favourable to China's peaceful development."

Paper also states that "Developing all-round military-to-military relations, China's armed forces will further their exchanges and cooperation with the *Russian military* within the framework of the comprehensive strategic partnership of coordination between China and Russia, and foster a comprehensive, diverse and sustainable framework to promote military relations in more fields and at more levels."

Another view on the White Paper

However, there are counterviews to the White Paper (July 2019). Scholars have felt that though the latest Chinese Defence White Paper brings out a picture of a People's Liberation Army being on its way to modernisation, documenting where progress has or has not been achieved in its mammoth military reform efforts. The seasoned readers of the Chinese Defence

White Papers would see many commonalities between the earlier and the latest 24 July version. However, some notable differences and developments are discernibly glaring (Nouwens 2019).

Keeping in line with the 2015 document, the July 2019 paper focuses on regional challenges to China's national security. The paper highlights the fact that as of now China remains to be a regional military actor, still falling short of being a global one. The White Paper has predictably castigated the United States as the source of regional and global instability through its military alliances, deployment and intervention, hegemony and 'significantly increased' defence expenditure.

The 2015 paper 'explained' China's military strategy and outlined the direction that military reforms would take. Notably, the strategy outlined in 2015 still holds more or less true, with specific attention paid to China's No First Use nuclear policy.

But the 2019 paper has surprisingly added a new section dedicated to 'reasonable and appropriate defence expenditure', arguing that China spends less on its military than the US, United Kingdom, Japan, Germany or France. But the picture of actual expenditure, though slightly clarified, still remains murky.

What is left out of the White Paper?

Nouwens (Nouwens 2019a) has rightly pointed out that:

> "Also of interest would be not only what has been included but more so what has been left out of the 2019 White Paper." Since 2015 there has been significant open-source

> reporting on China's development of advanced equipment and platforms. In the White Paper, only one example is given for each service branch: the Type-15 tank for the Army, Type-052D destroyer for the Navy, J-20 fighter for the Air Force and DF-26 for the Rocket Force. But it does not make any mention of developments relating to hypersonic cruise missiles or glide vehicles, uninhabited aerial vehicles or the air-launched or sea-launch nuclear-capable missiles that China continues to develop. Similarly, nuanced discussions on the organisation of the Strategic Support Force and Rocket Force are missing".

Interestingly, the 'Belt and Road Initiative' (BRI) also does not find a mention in the July 2019 document, though attention has been paid to. But the paper highlights the usage of the People's Armed Police (now governed by the Central Military Commission of the Chinese Communist Party), for combating terrorism. The PLA has now been assigned the role to protect China's overseas interests through international security cooperation. However, using the above facts as definitive proof for China's plans to militarise the Belt and Road Initiative would be reading a bit far between the lines.

Analysis

China's white paper "*China's National Defence in the New Era* (July 2019), has evidently brought many aspects related to PLA preparations, regional strategies, Cooperation with Russia but leaving out many issues like BRI, which would need to be read in between the lines. All these actions would have an impact on India's national interests and security. It is, therefore, important that India studies the white paper thoroughly—also reading in between the lines—and prepares its own counter-strategies, to protect its national interests."

Russia's Military Strategy

Image Courtesy morefamousquotes.com (http://www.morefamousquotes.com/authors/georgy-zhukov-quotes/)

It has always been a mammoth task to decipher Russia's Military Strategy, Zhukov's words "There are things in Russia which are not as they seem", reflect on that fact. A report (CRS 2020) which was presented to Members of the US Congress explained the evolution and current state of Russian Military Doctrine and Strategy, to assess Russian intentions and capabilities.

The report brought out that Russia had expanded its military capabilities over the last decade, as seen through its invasion of Ukraine and intervention in Syria. Undoubtedly, the enhanced military capabilities have enabled the Russian government to expand its policy options and pursue more aggressive foreign policy decisions. These changes seem to in consonance with recent statements and adjustments to Russian military doctrine that clearly provide insights into Russian leaders' thinking related to the use of force for advancing Russia's foreign policy objectives. Russian Military and Security Strategy Documents and Russia's official security doctrines are detailed in its 2014 Military Doctrine and 2015 National Security Strategy.

Other key strategy documents include the 2016 Foreign Policy Concept, 2017 Naval Strategy, and 2020 Principles of Nuclear Deterrence Strategy. These documents offer insight into how Russian leaders perceive threats and how Russian military and security policymakers envision the future of conflict. In addition, the Military Doctrine and the National Security Strategy identify the importance of information and the danger of internal, as well as external, threats.

The 2014 Military Doctrine had divided the perceived nature of threats to Russia into two categories: military risks and military threats. Military risks are a lesser designation, defined as situations that could "lead to a military threat under certain conditions". On the other hand, a military threat has been characterised as a "real possibility of an outbreak of a military conflict". Once fighting breaks out, Russian military theory and doctrine identify a typology of conflicts relating to the extent and type of conflict, gradually increasing in intensity: armed conflict, local war, regional war, large-scale war, and global (nuclear) war.

The above levels of conflict are important for understanding how the Russian military envisions the scale, nature, actors, and levels of escalation in the war. Russian Security Council

Secretary Nikolay Patrushev, in July 2019, had stated that Russia would update its *National Security Strategy in 2020.* Although a new version has not yet appeared, most analysts expect its publication in the near future.

Unlike China, the Russian Document does not mention strategies for cooperation with any specific country. In best of its old traditions, Russia still seems to follow a compartmentalised approach even towards its Military Strategy (CRS 2020).

Need for Update of the Doctrine-2020

The reasons for updating the existing Russian doctrine have been analysed. Massicot (Massicot 2019) has pointed out that "There are a few reasons why the Russian military may release an updated doctrine in 2020". The pressing need for updated policy could be attributed to the hardening of Russian threat perception with respect to the United States, based on which Russia appears to be entering a cycle of updating several national security strategy documents.

The year 2020 has proven to be an important and crucial year for Russian military planning. It also appears as an ideal time for transitioning past the tumultuous, expensive, and difficult modernisation and readiness building work of the last decade. Since 2008, the Russian military has undertaken ambitious, 'New Look' reforms to—among other things—replace or modernise 70 per cent of its military equipment by 2020, increase the number of enlisted personnel, and overhaul the defence industrial base. In support of that Russia's Defence Minister Sergey Shoygu had said that he believed these reforms and a series of presidential decrees also tied to the year 2020 would allow the Russian military to "reach a new qualitative level" (Massicot 2019a). The full import of this Russian exercise is still emerging.

It has been seen that for the most part, their former efforts have been fairly successful. It is probable that the updated doctrine would mostly take into account the qualitative improvements in readiness and procurement of the last decade and would be an important signal of a new phase in military development by looking to the future—to 2030 and beyond.

The updated doctrine is also expected to take into account new approaches as Russian threat perceptions have hardened considerably since the last doctrine was released in 2014, particularly with respect to the United States and NATO. Russian leaders believe that certain negative trends—the use of economic sanctions, "colour revolutions," and the potential for interstate conflict—are accelerating. They assess that the current US-led world order would be coming to an end while rising powers like China, Russia, and others challenge the existing order. Senior officials assume Washington and its allies have been attempting to contain or intimidate Russia. They cite as evidence the latest *National Defence Strategy* and *Nuclear Posture Review*, the Pentagon's renewed focus on great power competition, and NATO's rotational troop presence in Eastern Europe. Some of the languages in an updated military doctrine may reflect this growing pessimism. Deepening distrust of the West was a prominent feature of the 2015 Russian *National Security Strategy* and 2016 *Foreign Policy Concept* and may show influence on the anticipated 2020 Strategy document (ibid.).

In the final analysis, from a purely bureaucratic standpoint, it's seemingly an opportune time for presenting an updated military doctrine to the world. It has been seen that over the last two years, the Russian government has been busy updating multiple strategy documents related to national security and domestic policy issues. As a matter of record, the previous two Russian military doctrines were published in 2010 and 2014, as part of a constellation of several other national security-related strategies, most of which were written to last 'until the period of 2020'. Thus it's not surprising that the Secretary of the Russian Federation Security Council Nikolay Patrushev, in July 2019, had pointed out that Russia would update its '*National Security Strategy*' in the year 2020.

In fact, it was predicted that an updated military doctrine could be released as early as late December 2019, at the poetic dawn of a new decade. However, the COVID-19 pandemic seems to have delayed the exercise (RCS 2020/Bowen 2020).

Nine Things to Look for in the New Doctrine

In relation to the 'New Russian Doctrine' Massicot (2019a) has brought out that:

> "In general, the language and structure of Russia's military doctrines tend to be stable from one version to the next. However, small changes are often significant—additions and subtractions to the document reflect larger programmatic changes, points of emphasis, and clues about future activities. For example, internal threats were included for the first time in the 2014 doctrine, and since then Russia updated the legal relationships between the military and internal security agencies, created the National Defence Control Centre in Moscow

to better monitor and respond to many types of threats, and consolidated multiple internal security services into the national guard (*rosgvardia*). In another example, the 2016 *Russian Foreign Policy Concept* deleted references to the INF Treaty, a subtle foreshadowing of the agreement's implosion this year."

An analysis based on Russian threat perceptions, leadership statements, force modernisation, and combat operations since the last military doctrine's publication in 2014; the following points are likely to be included in a new Russian military doctrine (Massicot 2019a):

- A continued emphasis on non-military methods before and during military conflict
- The strategy of active defence
- The strategy of limited action
- Congested battlefields and the growing role of private military company
- The uneasy future of arms control
- No major revisions to the declared nuclear-use policy
- The importance of emerging classes of weapons, combat robotics, and artificial intelligence
- Coded barbs against the US with a focus on great power competition
- The United States would probably not be upgraded into the "military threat" category

Gerasimov's Legacy

The updated military doctrine 2020 is expected to bear an indelible mark of Gerasimov—currently the Chief of the

General Staff. The United States and its allies have been advised to anticipate reflection of Gerasimov's legacy in an updated Russian military doctrine expected in 2020. Evaluating this document closely—particularly changes in tone or shifts in content from previous versions—would be important for understanding Russian threat perceptions and the leadership's methods to address those threats. Russia's military doctrines contain explicit and implicit signalling, and any new document will likely reflect Russia's deepening pessimism and concerns with instability in the international order. An updated doctrine is also expected to prioritise new capabilities like hypersonic missiles, combat robotics, artificial intelligence, and a growing sophistication in melding military and non-military tools to achieve results (Massicot 2019b).

Common Thread between China's and Russia's Military Strategies

It would not be very difficult to find a common thread between the Military Strategies of China and Russia based on the dictum 'Enemy's Enemy is my Friend'. In reference to the Sino-Russia Military Pact, President Putin had said "The time will show how it will develop, but we won't exclude it ... indicating the direction in which the Sino-Russia relationship is moving.

In his detailed analysis of Sino-Russian strategies *Kuczyński* (2019) corroborated the above thought by pointing out "Over the last decades, Moscow and Beijing have strengthened their military relationship. This cooperation has been mainly based not on collective visions, but rather on shared fears. It is hard to resist the impression that the only factor bringing the two countries closer is their common enemy."

Kuczyński also stated that:

> "What brought Russia and China together has been mainly their rivalry with the United States. There has been, however, a significant difference between the two in their perspective in this race. Russia treats this at political and military levels and China—primarily at economics and trade levels. This difference may, in the long run, prove to be a major factor influencing Beijing's cooperation with Moscow."

It has been observed that between the two countries (China and Russia), Moscow has been more interested in tightening their cooperation or even building a Sino-Russian alliance. A weakening Russia sees its partnership with Beijing as a solution against Washington's global domination. Russia began to speak out about forming a partnership with Beijing shortly after it became clear that the reset policy towards the United States was coming to an end.

It has also been observed that over the last three decades, Russia and China have significantly developed their military cooperation (arms sales, joint military exercises, among others). The advanced weapons provided by Moscow have allowed China to strengthen its air defence and anti-ship defence. In particular, they have enhanced China's capability to defend against the threat of foreign naval and air forces near its territory. Participation in joint exercises with Russia has also allowed China to learn from Russian combat experiences gained, in Ukraine or Syria.

2. Sino-Russia Strategic Partnership and Probability of Joint Military Pact

Status

The current cooperation between the Russian Federation and the People's Republic of China has become the most intense since the two countries signed their Treaty of Friendship in 2001. Kuczyński (2019a) has opined that "Although Putin's regime has never treated China as its enemy, Moscow's long-lasting priority originating in the Yeltsin era was its cooperation with the West". However, the situation changed with Putin transforming Russia's policy towards the West and making it confrontational. On the other hand, when the United States became aware of the perilously growing potential of China—already far beyond exclusively economic issues, the USA also changed its strategies towards China, which certainly had an impact on Russia and Asia. Though Russia made a turn towards Asia at the beginning of Putin's third term in office, it began actively promoting a 'privileged strategic partnership' with China since 2014 (Kuczyński 2019a).

The actual cooperation between China and Russia picked up momentum after the two countries concluded a significant gas deal ('Power of Siberia' pipeline project). Further, as Russia's relationship with the West deteriorated, after its aggression in Ukraine, China became Moscow's top priority. Based on that, China started developing its Eurasian strategy—with Russia as its crucial element. In addition to access to cheap energy supplies, close ties with Russia (a weaker neighbour) offered Beijing an opportunity to develop its investments and political influence in the region, and, above all, to strengthen its position against the US.

As a matter of record, in November 2014, Russia had openly invited Beijing to form a military alliance (with Russia's Defence Minister Sergei Shoigu and his deputy Anatoly Antonov speaking of the joint fight against terrorism and 'colour revolutions'). But China, for a considerably long time, did not find this idea lucrative. China began to open up more to military cooperation with Russia, only after the relationship of the former with the US began to worsen after Donald Trump came to power. It fit in well with the increasingly forceful, global and expansive foreign policy pursued by China's President Xi Jinping.

In 2019, cooperation between the two countries reached the next stage and continued to become more intense. Both countries realise that the development of mutual military cooperation which would "enrich the strategic partnership between China and Russia in the new era" would play a significant role in maintaining global strategic stability." The 2019 China's White Paper makes a clear reference to this fact. The above analysis has been facilitated by many scholarly reviews on the subject including that of Kuczyński.

Analysis

In view of the above facts, it is opined that the ground for the "Sino-Russia Military Pact" is now quite fertile.

Counter View based on Sino-Russian Disagreements

There are always views and counter views. It is important to examine both for arriving at a balanced analysis. There has been a certain scepticism about the Sino-Russian Military Pact. The issue will be examined in the succeeding paragraphs.

Warsaw Institute Review (WIR 2019) special Study report has opined that the US has been concerned about the increasing Sino-Russian closeness. It has referred to the Director of National Intelligence's (Coats) observation that China and Russia were more aligned than at any point since the mid-1950s. Nevertheless, compared to the diplomatic and economic aspects, the military aspects of the Sino-Russian partnership were still relatively weak enough to make it impossible for Moscow and Beijing to forge an alliance. Coats (ibid.) had further stated that the participation of Chinese armed forces in the Vostok-2018 and *Tsentr 2019* military training activities should not be overestimated. Notably, Russia deployed several hundred thousand troops and about a thousand aircraft, China sent a fraction—3200 soldiers and six aircraft.

However, a classic full-fledged alliance between China and Russia in the near future has been ruled out because it would be based solely on their rivalry with the US—perceived differently in Moscow and Beijing. Besides, there are many differences between the two countries—among others, the rivalry in the Arctic and the North Pacific, the two regions that Russia seeks to guard against competitors (China has grown 'polar' ambitions) and selling Russian weapons to Beijing's biggest rival, India, and also to Vietnam (WIR 2019).

Another field of silent competition between Russia and China touches Central Asia, the fact of which can be observed within the framework of the Shanghai Cooperation Organisation. Russia wants the SCO to remain purely military and limited to defence, while China would like to transform it into a more comprehensive body, a tool for developing economic influence in the post-Soviet area.

It has been observed that the end of the Russian-American INF treaty may open a way for the deployment of intermediate-range missiles near China also by its main continental neighbour. The missile arsenal of China has long been a factor taken into account by Russian strategists. The development of modernised and more precise Chinese intermediate-range ballistic missiles (IRBMs) was one of the reasons why Russia began threatening to leave the INF as early as 2007.

Another important and notable factor which has been observed relates to the fact that Beijing did not endorse the annexation of Crimea by Russia and its factual annexation of Abkhazia and South Ossetia, while Moscow does not provide formal diplomatic support for Chinese claims in the South China Sea and the East China Sea. Both Moscow and Beijing want to avoid being drawn into conflicts with third countries by the other side. The above analysis has been based on CRS 2020 and WIR 2019 reports.

The above views have been corroborated by Nurlan (2020). He has stated that:

> while both sides seek to avoid describing the current partnership as an alliance, military cooperation between Russia

> and China has increased in recent years and in reality, there are some striking signs of a military alliance. They conduct joint exercises, hold regular and extensive talks and conduct educational projects for each other's military staff, but do not wish to form a formal alliance.

Thus, there is discernible scepticism about referring to China and Russia's relationship as a military alliance, as of now.

Analysis

After going through the differing opinions, the author feels that a strategic "Military Pact" between China and Russia has become more of a necessity. With the embroilment of China in many disputes simultaneously, including Ladakh and the South China Sea, the USA's hardening stance and weakened economic situation of Russia, both countries (China and Russia) would like to avoid tension between them and would also like to have a joint strategy to contain the USA; thus *a Sino-Russia Military Pact"* seems very likely. Not a very palatable situation for India.

Probable Scope of the Sino-Russia Military Pact

After establishing a high probability for the conclusion of the Sino-Russia Military Pact, it would be essential to analyse its likely contents.

Current Status

The Russia-China military relationship has been seen to evolve, as a logical progression of their deepening political, defence and economic ties. Kuczyński (2020b) in his article related to Sino-Russian relations have pointed out that

> "Paradoxically, an analysis of aspects related to the restoration of the arms trade, joint exercises, and military patrols, would show how Sino-Russian cooperation has been delayed in the context of documents and formal agreements. The Treaty of Good-Neighbourliness and Friendly Cooperation between the People's Republic of China and the Russian Federation signed on July 16, 2001, did not include a defence clause in which both parties would undertake to provide military assistance in the event of aggression by a third country. The document, however, while allowing a window for defence cooperation, does not give a possibility for joint military action against a third country. The said window for defence cooperation has a linkage to a 1993 agreement between China and Russia."

China and Russia had signed an agreement (between the defence minister of China and Russia) on October 11, 1993. The relatively short and general document had its focus on creating conditions for cooperation in the area of military technologies of the two countries. It mentioned training of personnel, exchange of experience and information, mutual assistance in servicing weapons and military equipment, and joint scientific and historical military events.

The said 1993 document interestingly did not provide for joint military exercises but mentioned inviting representatives of the other country to exercises as guests. The document did, nonetheless, leave room for other forms of cooperation by adding a provision that they are "subject to agreement between the parties, As a result, by December 1 of each year, the two countries would sign a cooperation plan for the following year, detailing the steps for developing mutual cooperation. Sometimes additional agreements were signed, such as the 2007 agreement on the status of troops temporarily stationed on each other's territory—which was made after regular joint exercises started to be organised in 2005. In 2017, a three-year roadmap was adopted, providing a legal basis for a wide range of forms of military cooperation between China and Russia.

The author acknowledges immense assistance from an article by Kuczyński (2020b) in carrying out the above factual analysis. The analysis clearly shows that China-Russia has had ever-growing cooperation in defence matters since 1993. But now—with a fast-changing geo-politico-economic situation in the region—both countries are feeling the heat and are seeing the need for entering into a formal "Military Pact".

What to Expect?

It is anticipated that all of the existing agreed activities, as well as plans for the next ones, would most certainly find a mention in the new military cooperation agreement—replacement of the outdated 1993 deal. The Sino-Russian Treaty of Friendship, which also would soon expire—in 2021—is expected to be renewed. It cannot be ruled out that the new document would include provisions concerning the joint defence of China and Russia. This may turn out to be the most accurate indication of the actual level of military cooperation between the two countries and, last but not least, of the intentions of their leaders for the future.

WIR (2020) based on its study on the subject has observed that it's only recently, Russia has started using the word 'ally' to refer to China. One of such first public uses was a comment of the Kremlin spokesperson Dmitry Peskov on the Chinese participation in the Russian strategic exercises Vostok-2018: "It is a sign of the expanded partnership between the two sides in all spheres." In June 2019, the Russians described the agreements, including one for military cooperation, signed by Putin and Xi in Moscow as the opening of a 'new era,' for both the countries.

The statements made by Russia (with Putin at the forefront) mirrored a new level of military partnership—a kind of "undeclared alliance." Russia wants to develop military cooperation with China in specific areas: in the air and at sea —which is visibly directed against the US At the same time, Moscow does not want to hurry with supporting China in modernising its land forces—the element of military potential that could threaten Russia in the future.

The June 2019 'Joint Statement on Developing a Comprehensive Partnership of Strategic Coordination for a New Era,' stated that while developing their bilateral relations, Russia and China 'refused to forge an alliance, to confront and to act against third countries'. The joint statement did mention a 'strategic alliance' that does not, however, contain the firm commitment to provide military assistance, if one of the allies becomes a target. Although it is worth adding that the still valid Article 9 of the 2001 Sino-Russian Treaty of Good-Neighbourliness and Friendly Cooperation states: "When a situation arises in which one of the contracting parties deem that peace is being threatened and undermined or its security interests are involved, or when it is confronted with the threat of aggression, the contracting parties shall immediately hold contacts and consultations in order to eliminate such threats.

The Missile rapprochement and Arctic Arms Treaty between the two countries are other important elements expected to be covered by the Pact. The above analysis has been based on inputs from the article in the Warsaw Institute Review (WIR 2020a).

Corroborating the above view, Sardzhyan and Flood (2019) have quoted Zwack as saying: "The Russia-China military relationship would be important for China. The PLA [China's army], which hasn't seen a war since its brusque 1979 defeat by Vietnam, hopes to learn from Russia's newly gained fighting expertise, derived since 2014 in eastern Ukraine and Syria. It will be crucial to determine if their interaction evolves more ominously into interoperability exercises where substantial and varied forces can operate in tandem and jointly in coordinated operations.

Sardzhyan and Flood's analysis has indicated that while vulnerable to potential future problems including an increasing resource imbalance ... both nations have bigger fish to fry. Russia's issues to the west and south, and in China's case, in the southeast Pacific, *and with India to a lesser extent* have forced both the countries to keep their own borders calm and have a more insulated trading relationship.... It would also be important to note that the need for making increased military interaction more attractive emerges from a shared perception that the United States and its allies are determinately blocking Sino-Russian more autocratic aspirations and directly threatening their regimes. It's a fact these two countries neither have major allies nor are they part of a well-organised security alliance like NATO. They are loath about being internationally isolated or contained, which explains why both, even while pursuing different agenda[s], are usually in lockstep with each other on major security issues in the UN and other international fora."

Analysis

The details stated above bring out the precarious geo-politico-economic situation of China and Russia, With China facing considerable wrath from the world (for its belligerence in the South China Sea, its Maritime boundary disputes with neighbouring countries and objecting to lawful freedom of navigation in the South China Sea) needs a strong ally to safeguard its interests, and similarly economically ravaged Russia needs a friend in the backyard—worth it's salt. Thus a "Sino-Russia Military Pact" seems to be just a matter of time.

3. Implications for India

Analysis of an unavoidable impact on India of the "Sino-Russia Military Pact" would form the crux of this monograph. That would warrant examination of Indo-China/Indo-Russia Relations/Efficacy of RIC/Indo-US relations/QUAD and entwined linkages.

Review of Indo-China Relationship

Historically, India and China have had sustained relations for more than 2,000 years, but the era of the modern relationship began in 1950. Reddy (2016) has stated in his article that the first records of contact between China and India were written during the 2nd century BCE. China and India have also had some contact before the transmission of Buddhism from India to China in the 1st century CE. References to a race called the Chinas, now believed to be the Chinese, have been found in ancient Indian literature. The Indian epic Mahabharata (c. 5th century BCE) contains references to "China", which may have been referring to the Qin state which later became the Qin Dynasty. Chanakya (c. 350-283 BCE), the Prime Minister of the Maurya Empire and a Professor at Takshashila University, referred to Chinese silk as "cinamsuka" (Chinese silk dress) and "cinapatta" (Chinese silk bundle) in his Arthashastra. Vijay Gokhale, Indian Ambassador to China, also observed that "even before the transmission of Buddhism, the Shang-Zhou civilisation and the ancient Vedic civilisation in 1500-

1000 BC showed some evidence of conceptual and linguistic exchanges.

Cultural exchanges between India and China continued during the days of India's struggle for self-governance. In the early 20th century, Nobel laureate Rabindranath Tagore visited China twice, in 1924 and 1929; while scholars and intellectuals since 1911 have been visiting and revisiting Tagore's life, works and philosophy.

These records would seem good enough to glorify the historical and cultural ties between India and China. But on the other side of the coin, China and India viewed as the 'Emerging Giants' have also stood facing security challenges—'old' and 'new' tensions, the former stemming from historical territorial disputes and the latter from mounting economic, military and political rivalries. China has more clout than India in South and Southeast Asia, as could be discernible from the intensification of China's ties with Myanmar, Bangladesh and Sri Lanka.

However, India is gradually making its presence felt in this sub-region. To enhance its influence, India launched in the 1990s its Look East Policy which has increasingly focussed on security issues in Southeast Asia, notwithstanding China's prominence. In South Asia, India has wielded more influence than China which has however been making inroads into countries such as Pakistan, Nepal, Sri Lanka and Bangladesh. There are some 'Old' tensions rooted in territorial disputes. These relate to conflict over Tibet in the 1950s and deep suspicion over rival claims—India's over Aksai Chin and China's over Arunachal Pradesh. Despite the rhetoric of friendship, mutual suspicions and anxieties can frustrate their long term relationship. Alongside, surprises and doubts arise from India's relationship with Pakistan, and China's support for the latter along with India's Kashmir and China's claims over Xinjiang province and Arunachal Pradesh, along India's North East and Tibet's South. Sadly, the war between China and India in 1962 and the breakdown of relations between the two nations shattered Jawaharlal Nehru's 'Asian dream'.

If China wants to see the rise of a peaceful and creative Asian century, it will have to seriously and demonstratively deviate from the present course. Muni (Muni 2016) has opined that China would need to deal—peacefully and sensitively—with Tibet and the Dalai Lama and his people so as to accommodate their aspirations and culture. Once that is done, a great deal of the resolution of the India-China border dispute will fall in place through confidence building and peaceful negotiations. China also needs to learn to honour the aspirations and give appropriate space to its neighbouring countries rather than going into hegemonic mode.

China cannot ever deny that India has always followed a policy of defence, whereas China has always followed a policy of aggression. It does not hesitate to use military force to meet political gains. In fact, the then Chinese Premier Zhou Enlai went on to say that the only reason why China went on to war with India was to "teach India a lesson". In the same manner, they attacked Vietnam to "teach it a lesson, just like India". It's this aggressionist policy that has managed to instil fear among China's neighbours. India, on the other hand, has never used force; the principle of non-violence has been deeply ingrained in India's ideologies and forms a cornerstone of its foreign policy.

It is important that concrete steps need to be taken by China to ensure that this objective is achieved. China needs to accept that a cordial relationship with India would not only be important for both countries, but also for the sake of regional stability in South Asia. The above views have also been corroborated by Gokhale (2020).

India's Continual Misreading of China's Intentions

India has more often than not has misread China—generally paying for it considerably. India has, for some reason, has found it difficult to accept that China has been the most unreliable friend to work with, who would not hesitate to stab India in the back. If it serves China's interest better.

India, by and large, has been a silent spectator to continual actions of China related to modernisation of PLA, development of border infrastructure, encircling of India by trapping neighbouring countries in deadly Debt Traps, incursions on land (Arunachal Pradesh/Dok La/Eastern Ladakh), and operations in IOR and near Andaman and Nicobar Islands. The current hard stance of India against China (though very surprising for China compared to Indian culture of lodging strong protests or issuing 'Note Verbale's), however, seems to be too little too late.

Dey, A 2020 has tweaked—"*War is a mere continuation of policy with other means*—Clausewitz's (Prussian general and military theorist) eternal definition of war a little, and stated that from the geopolitical and military strategy of the People's Republic of China it is evident that 'Local' war is a mere continuation of 'geopolitics' with other means—has become the guiding principle of China under President Xi Jinping".

In fact, China's 2013 defence white paper was a precursor to Xi's intentions, specific emphasis on the modernisation of the People's Liberation Army (PLA), an alarm on the increasing US presence in the Indo-Pacific, and special mention of Taiwan and Tibet in the 2015 document. The document, released after Xi was elected president in 2013, stated the PLA would "win local wars under the conditions of informationisation"—the increased use of information technology in short localised wars.

The writing was on the wall in 2015. But in traditional Pakistan-obsession and trust in Chinese Bonhomie (as usual now proven fake) the Indian governments probably did not interpret, with due seriousness, the situation at Line of Actual Control (LAC) in general, and the 2015 Defence White Paper in particular.

The current Ladakh imbroglio and the past incursions by Beijing in the freezing heights, the increasing Chinese belligerence towards Hong Kong and Taiwan in recent years, and the continuous fierce military expansion in the oil and the gas-rich South China Sea have their roots in China's 2015 White Paper on Defence.

Misinterpretation of China's 2015 White Paper and Transformation of PLA

Dey (2020a) went on to say "The 2015 China's White Paper on Defence and related documents were completely ignored by New Delhi, as it probably did not realise the significance." The paper had tasked the PLA to "resolutely safeguard the unification of the motherland". To jog India's memory, Mao Zedong considered Tibet China's right palm and intended to liberate—rather, unite—its fingers: Ladakh, Nepal, Sikkim, Bhutan and the North-East Frontier Agency (now Arunachal Pradesh).

The paper showed that China would focus on cyber and space warfare and joint military operation; develop "long-range, precise, smart, stealthy and unmanned weapons"; and prioritise local and "Informationisation" wars as "in the foreseeable future, a world war is unlikely".

The 2019 China's White Paper though based on similar principles as the 2015 Paper, it went much farther. In that, the 2019 White Paper is more explicit, speaks of action in more concrete terms and makes a specific reference to enhanced military cooperation with Russia. A sign India can ignore at its own peril.

Major Chinese Future Threats Ignored

Local informationised war: Dey (2020a) had said that "Around four decades ago, Deng Xiaoping had predicted the unlikeliness of major wars or nuclear attacks; instead, he foresaw local wars—for example, the Kargil War—and wanted the PLA to transform accordingly. His successor, Jian Zemin, called for the PLA's transformation to win such wars under modern technology and preferring quality to quantity—as implemented by Xi."

Had India launched a military offensive against the PLA in eastern Ladakh after the Galwan River Valley clash, it would have been a "local informationised war" fought by China—geographically limited, speedy, short, with rapid integration and mobilisation of forces, highly destructive using lethal weapons and using C4ISR (command, control, communications, computers, intelligence, surveillance and reconnaissance). China would have also used its anti-satellite (ASAT) weapons, and electromagnetic pulse (EMP) attacks to cripple India's weapons command and control systems, power and communications grids, and integrated cyber-attacks that can hack our banks, government institutions and our emails. It would be a platform-integrated war with PLAGF, PLA Navy, PLA Air Force, PLA Rocket Force and PLASSF networked closely. Proving the fact "... *the* [Chinese] *armed forces will adhere to the principles of flexibility, mobility and self-dependence so that 'you fight your way and I fight my way'*," as said in that document.

Based on the previous experience, India needs to avoid making the same mistake of ignoring the latest White Paper. As pointed out by Nouwens (Nouwens 2019b) "The latest Chinese Defence White Paper released on July 24, 2019 paints a picture of a People's Liberation Army that is on its way to modernising, documenting where progress has, or has not, been made in military reform efforts ..., and achieving its objectives."

Analysis

The above analysis would ring the bells all over as it points out unfathomable apathy by India towards China's historical unpredictability, a country whose actions can have an indelible and disastrous mark on the future of India.

Need for India's Cautious Approach to China

India needs to shade its apathy and shore up and execute its counters to China's belligerence, albeit with Caution.

Bhattacharya (2004) has pointed out that "Interestingly Jawaharlal Nehru had regarded China as a threat for he felt Indian and Chinese cultures had been contesting for supremacy for hundreds of years in Central Asia, Tibet, Burma and the countries of Southeast Asia. Indeed, India and China are two geopolitical rivals and their interests' clash—both in the political and economic arena. Both are vying for the same markets. India calls the Central Asian region it's 'extended neighbourhood' while to China it is the 'strategic backyard'.

Political analysts have also talked about a new flashpoint between India and China in ASEAN. Both view the Southeast Asian region as an important market and crucial to their security concerns. In Sudan, China is already playing a proactive role. Recently, India entered the oil sector of Sudan. Militarily both are building their blue-water capability. While India is attempting to project its naval power through the Indian Ocean and has conducted joint military exercises with the US in the Malacca Straits to the chagrin of China, China is trying to penetrate the Indian Ocean through Myanmar much to the alarm of India. Given this clash of interests between China and India, it is highly unlikely for them to have strong mutual relationships. In addition, China's belligerence in the South China Sea is a big impediment in India's Look East and Act East policies.

Pakistan is yet another major irritant in India-China relations. China is not likely to give up its strategic alliance with Pakistan. It is China's primary card to block India from emerging as a great Asian power. By playing the Pakistan card, China seeks to keep India embroiled in South Asia. China's ambition of great power status is not only contingent on a strong economy as it is widely known but also on its diplomacy of keeping India tied to the South Asian region. China maintains a fine balance between India and Pakistan so that Pakistan is checked from being too reckless and India does not pose a challenge to it. China's aid to Pakistan has not been confined only to the transfer of nuclear technology and arms sales. It has brought its Belt and Road Initiative (BRI) to India's back yard through the development of the strategic Gwadar port with the financial assistance of US$ 248 million.

Leaving aside Pakistan, the border issue has been another equally thorny issue for India-China relations. Despite regular JWG meetings and a series of ministerial interactions, there has been no progress in resolving the border issue. Therefore, India can't afford to remain apathetic to China—and has to act decisively. The author would like to quote here Sun Tzu "*If your enemy is secure at all points, be prepared for him. If he is in superior strength, evade him. If your opponent is temperamental, seek to irritate him. Pretend to be weak, that he may grow arrogant. If he is taking his ease, give him no rest. If his forces are united, separate them. If sovereign and subject are in accord, put a division between them. Attack him where he is unprepared, appear where you are not expected.*" India seems to have been successful in doing that in the Galwan Valley.

It would also be very important to note that post clashes in the Easter Ladakh region of India (Galwan Valley) and loss of face suffered by China; it has been trying to create problems for India on multiple fronts. Using Taiwan as an excuse, China has warned India that it would support the insurgency in India if India does not refrain from supporting Taiwan. Lintner (2020) has quoted Long Xingchun, president of the Chengdu Institute of World Affairs, as "Once a country wants to develop official trade ties [with Taiwan], it is by no means a pure trade issue." He followed with a stern if not ominous warning: "If India supports Taiwan secessionist forces, China and India will come to hostility, especially if India's moves (sic.) force China to support secessionist forces in India as a countermeasure. Each would attack the weakness of the other". This could also point to the revival of old links between Nagas and China.

In the opinion of Pant (2020), "By all reckoning, this has been a dramatic year. With two more months to go, it has already shattered a number of assumptions about global politics and its emerging trend lines. For Indian foreign policy, this year has been full of vexing challenges as well, and it has forced Indian policymakers to make some decisive shifts in their engagement with the outside world, in particular where it concerns China".

Chinese aggression has made it impossible for New Delhi to continue with its usual 'engagement where possible' refrain because there are hardly any areas where engagement seems possible between the two Asian neighbours. From trade and technology and Taiwan and Tibet, every aspect of their bilateral engagement seems to be in play at the moment.

These signs need to be taken seriously by India as such belligerent behaviour of China does not behove well for bilateral relations. India, therefore, needs to be prepared to contain China using all available—diplomatic-economic-strategic-security—means.

Some Measures India needs to take for Containment of China

India's appeasement policy towards China has met its inevitable, tragic denouement. But as inevitable and tragic as this was, it will be compounded if India hesitates, yet again, to respond with clarity and purpose. Until now, every Chinese signal that the northern neighbour was engaged in a containment strategy against India, has been ignored by New Delhi. It no longer should be the case.

Rajagopalan (2020) has stated in his analysis that "China must be contained not just because it has killed Indian soldiers, or prevented India's entry in the Nuclear Suppliers Group, or of the countless ways in which it has attempted to contain India. It must be contained because China won't stop doing any of this. It will not stop escalating on the Line of Actual Control (LAC), or containing India, or attacking its neighbours. Containing China is not a choice, but simply the lack of it."

Rajagopalan (2020) has recommended that India needs to focus on the following factors and accordingly frame its "China Containment Strategy":

- China's power must be set against its disadvantages. It has antagonised most of its neighbours. Its coercive use of trade against countries, near and far, has not only raised concerns but started an embryonic movement in many countries to limit their vulnerability. While Japan is paying its companies to relocate out of China, the US is considering an Economic Prosperity Network of trusted trade partners.

- Its aggression against India follows its forcible takeover of the South China Sea, brushing aside the claims of others. China demonstrates neither moderation nor self-interested pragmatism. This is a critical disadvantage that glues the coalition.
- China's geography is another disadvantage for Beijing. True, a large country with internal lines of communication have some advantages and create difficulties for coordinating action between countries as far away as Japan, Australia and India. However, China is also hemmed in by chokepoints controlled by others, a particularly critical disadvantage for a country that depends on trade, as much as China does. Coordination between different regional players can help control these chokepoints and cut them off, should such a need ever arise.

To add to the above, Chaudhary (2020) has reported that "Beijing's ambitious Belt and Road Initiative (BRI) hailed by Pakistan and supported through the China-Pakistan Economic Corridor (CPEC) has reportedly hit a new roadblock. Specific area of dispute pertains to Main Line-1 (ML-1).ML-1 is the biggest project under CPEC worth US$ 6.8 billion. Under ML-1, a 2,655-km railway line will connect Karachi in the South to Peshawar in the North of Pakistan.

It has been reported that China isn't keen on the "One percent interest rate" on the loan demanded by Islamabad, for financing the project. Reportedly, the project needs to be financed jointly by Beijing and Islamabad, where Pakistan will invest 10 per cent of the project cost as equity and China will extend 90 per cent in the form of a loan under CPEC. China's BRI has received backlash from western countries for this arrangement. The US has criticised the CPEC programme saying that it is neither transparent nor cost-efficient. It has further warned Pakistan that it is subjecting itself to expensive loans under China's Belt and Road Initiative (BRI) through which Beijing has pledged more than US$ 60 billion so far (Chaudhary 2020).

Issues as mentioned above should be effectively used by India to contain China, through appropriate means, to its own advantage. It is opined that India seriously needs to put its "China Containment Plan" in action, on topmost Priority, as it is facing a now or never situation now. India needs to tell the Chinese Strategists that they often forget that the age of teaching anyone a lesson is over. Unilateralism and military aggression against a large country like India determined to defend its sovereignty and territorial integrity at any cost, will simply not work (Chinoy 2021). In such a situation the best way forward would revolve around a constructive dialogue and meaningful negotiations.

Analysis

It is very important for India to be fully aware of China's moves on its borders, in the South China Sea, in IOR, in Arabian Sea (Belt and Road Initiative), China's problems with South-East Asian countries, and its problems with BRI and formulate a strong counter-strategy, to safeguard its own interest. Undoubtedly *Russia* would have a big and important role to play in this area.

India and Russia: Existing Treaty of Friendship

Very Foundation of Indo-Russia Friendship

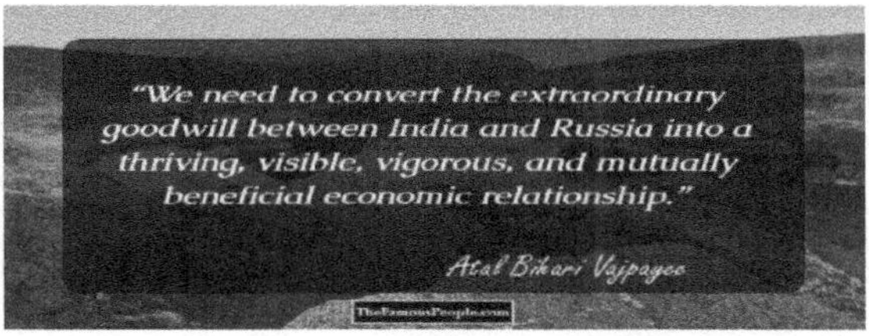

Image Courtesy famoupeople.com
https://quotes.thefamouspeople.com/atal-bihari-vajpayee-3649.php

The basic premise for Indo-Russia friendship has been well spelt by Former Prime Minister Atal Bihari Vajpayee's words and it also finds its roots in the preamble to the treaty (MEA Document August 1971):

> "DESIROUS of expanding and consolidating the existing relations of sincere friendship between them, BELIEVING that the further development of friendship and cooperation meets the basic national interests of both the States as well as the interests of lasting peace in Asia and the world, DETERMINED to promote the consolidation of universal peace and security and to make steadfast efforts for the relaxation international tensions and the final elimination of the remnants of colonialism, UPHOLDING their firm faith in the principles of peaceful coexistence and cooperation between States with different political and social systems, CONVINCED that in the world today international problems can only be solved by cooperation and not by conflict, REAFFIRMING their determination to abide by the purposes and principles of the United Nations Charter,

The Republic of India on one side, and The Union of Soviet Socialist Republic on the other side, HAVE decided to conclude the present Treaty...."

The gist of Indo-Russia Friendship Treaty

Trust and mutual interests have been at the base of India's relationship with the former Soviet Union, now the Russian federation.

In the years after its Independence, India gained industrially from the USSR which provided a base for its future growth. Starting in the 1950s, India received from the Soviet Union generous assistance for its industrialisation. Its development in the areas of defence, space and atomic energy had Soviet capital and knowhow. India was short of capital, foreign exchange and technology; the Soviet Union filled the gaps in India's development story letting India pay for projects in rupees through a special arrangement.

India got reliable, affordable and good quality military supplies and crucial products like oil and oil products, fertilisers, metals, etc. India's emerging Public Sector (PSUs) was scripted with Soviet help. India's relationship with USSR helped India in many ways to become more self-reliant.

It is important to note that the growing strategic dimensions of the India-Russia bilateral relationship have been grounded in the foundations of converging security interests at the global and regional levels. India supports Russia's call for multi-polarity, multilateralism and reforms in the UN Security Council. Russia supports India's candidature for a seat in the Security Council (UNSC) as India seeks a greater role for itself in the international system.

Weigold (2019) has commented on this treaty as seen through the western world's eyes. The key points mentioned by him are:

- Indo-Russian contact goes back to Nehru's first visit to Soviet Russia in the 1930s.
- Moves by the Western allies—SEATO, the Baghdad Pact and US-Pakistan relations—pushed non-aligned India towards China in 1954 and the Soviet Union in 1955, when exchange visits took place.
- The Sino-Indian war (1962) and the Indo-Pakistani wars in 1965 and 1971 furthered the Indo-Russian relationship.
- The Indo-Russian Treaty of Peace, Friendship and Co-operation (1971) was viewed with concern by the Western powers.
- The Indo-Russian relationship has been challenged in recent times by India's growing links with the US, but President Trump's June 2019 termination of the US preferential trade status for India has brought a new element to their bilateral relationship.
- Under a more "India First" second Modi government, India may be provoked into reassessing where its best interests lie.

Analysis

From the above it is clear India-Russia has a strong thread of mutual faith, respect and long-term friendship binding them. Given the current geopolitical and economic conditions, India cannot afford to lose time tested strong ally-Russia.

Why India needs Russia?

Undeniably India has been encircled by China by Proxy through neighbouring countries, entrapping them under unforeseen debt burden. The apparent threats from China's 'Belt and Road Initiative' (BRI News 2019) and CEPC cannot be ignored by India.

Though India is trying its best through its Look East Policy (LEP) and Act East Policy (AEP), it has been able to achieve only limited success, as India cannot wield the equivalent of China's Financial or Military might.

Thus being almost left alone to fend for itself India (the USA so far being only a fair-weather friend) certainly needs an all-weather friend like Russia, to protect its national interests.

From a deeper analysis of the Indo-Russia relationship, it would be evident that though not all the aspects of India's relationship with Russia have been smooth—it was abandoning its unique non-alignment policy to enter the Soviet camp, has been a subtle backbone to Indo-Russian long-term relations. The Indo-Russia relationship extends from leader-to-leader meetings in 1955 to Soviet support for India in its war with China in 1962, and its role as the chosen mediator after the UN-induced ceasefire in the war between India and Pakistan in 1965. The Indo-Russian Treaty of Peace, Friendship and Co-operation, signed in 1971, which has withstood the test of time despite being viewed with suspicion by the Western powers. To its credit, India has largely remained un-swayed by many attempts by Washington to cajole and coerce India to fully ally with it (Weigold 2019a).

However, India had to change with the times, and circumstances have forced India to have a much stronger relationship with the USA. Still, India tries its best to ensure that the primacy of the Indo-Russia relationship is not jeopardised. Various studies have focused on India's ongoing time tested relations with Russia. The studies have generally acknowledged India's expanding strategic engagements with its long-time friend, Russia, in terms of advantage or threat to India's Indo-Pacific and the Middle East intentions. Weigold (2019a) has rightly pointed out that "Despite US disapproval, India's purchase of Russian military hardware continues, maybe sometimes sporadically, since 1962". Most recently, the American President's ending of India's preferential trade status, the effect of which is as yet unknown, and India's refusal to cancel the S-400 Air Defence System deal under pressure for the USA may help in further cementing the India-Russia relationship.

On the subject Dr Weigold (2019a) has gone on to say that:

> Surrounding such debates on the recent Indo-Russian relationship, a broad discussion has also examined the effect of India's decade-long growing relationship with the United States that emerged with the genesis of the Indo-US nuclear agreement in 2006. For both states, it was a defensive reaction to China's economic and geographic expansion that, for the US, was also an attempt to wean India away from its non-alignment principles. For India, it was an independent bilateral agreement that did not cool its relations with Russia.

It is generally seen that in the debates relating to Indo-Russia friendship, the very foundations of India's close to a

70-year long relationship with Russia are often overlooked. In this context, India's steadfast quests for the development of a mutually beneficial relationship with the Soviet Union, Prime Minister Nehru's decisive role in its establishment during the Cold War and a push forward by Prime Minister Indira Gandhi's terms in the office are some of the important factors to add background and context to such debates.

In summary, the Indo-Russian relationship, since 1955, has been an unbroken one which in general has not subjected India to any pressure to give up its non-aligned position. It has been ongoing and despite US persuasion, India has not drawn away from Russia as its main supplier of weaponry. While China and Russia are now drawing closer in their national and regional interests, Russia has repeatedly supported India against Chinese aggression. Thus it is in India's interest to maintain a strong multi-lateral (cultural-economical-political and military) relationship with Russia.

Analysis

It would be clear from the above that even though India has fairly successfully tried to improve its relationships with many countries (including the USA), it has never undermined the primacy of the Indo-Russia relationship. A stable and flourishing relationship with Russia will always be good for furthering India's multidimensional national interests. To support this view author would like to refer to a statement by Joshi (2019) "Prime Minister Modi has understood the value of India being a swing power in the Asia-Pacific region. While it needs the US to balance the rising Chinese power, it realises that joining the American camp formally would reduce India's value. On the other hand, by cooperating and maintaining its military ties with Russia, it would be able to enhance its bargaining power with the US and still maintain a semblance of being a Eurasian power as well."

Deciphering Indo-China Russia Relationships Conundrum

Russia-India-China (RIC) relationship is not easy to unravel. Given the complexities in India-China, India-Russia and Russia-China relationship it is not easy to find a common ground. These countries also have their individual aspirations which are in contrast with each other, bringing down the commonality. In addition, the belligerent nature of China has created many problems for India, which Russia has not been able to resolve, creating a drift. Thus any attempt to decipher this conundrum can at best just scratch the surface.

In the current global scenario, the United States (US) undeniably enjoys a superior position, relative to any other state in the world. This has not been palatable to many countries. As per Bhattacharya (2004a), an alternate idea of strategic triangle took root with the end of the Cold War when the US assumed the role of a global cop. The idea of the triangle raised much hope to build a multi-polar world that would enable the creation of a just and fair international economic and political order.

Interestingly, though ideas on the trilateral (RIC) cooperation emphasise that they are not directed against any third power, there is a discernible objective of creating a competing power centre against the US. But, all the three powers are economically dependent on the US and each of them is seeking to deepen its relationship with the US, knowing that none can afford to annoy the sole superpower.

Bhattacharya (2004a) has rightly pointed out that "It is Russia, which would gain the most in this strategic triangle". It would help Russia to check NATO's eastward expansion. As far as China she said that "From the very beginning, China has shown apathy to the idea of the strategic triangle. Its foreign policy objective is grounded on a strong sentiment of bilateralism".

She has concluded by stating that "In sum, the popularity of the strategic triangle is mainly at the Track-II level (as there is nothing much for India to gain from it). It is unlikely to seriously influence the official policy in New Delhi. India must not be swayed by Russia's rhetoric of the strategic triangle". This view holds true even to-date.

Further, with India's expanding ties with the US (which became necessary mainly because of China's unwarranted belligerence) both China and Russia have felt threatened and they have tightened their embrace to safeguard their interest, the US being the common factor. The QUAD's increasing activities have added to China's and Russia's discomfort.

Thus, even if the world has seen the emergence of such a "strategic triangle" through RIC, prospects of it becoming strong enough to counter the US have become quite low. This has also been because of the fact the US has more comprehensive ties with Russia, China and India than any two of them have between themselves. Moreover, the bilateral ties among the three states in question suffer from so much inconsistency, that much more effort would be required to bring them to the footing of a meaningful strategic relationship. Not only are

Russia, China and India too weak to balance the US power in any significant measure but also strategic differences, China's physical incursions in Indian territory, Russia's reluctance to stem it has impeded these countries to meaningfully converge, and become a power to reckon with.

To examine another view, Raghavan (2020) has said that:

> "The elephant in the RIC room is the Indo-Pacific. For India, it is a geographic space of economic and security importance, in which a cooperative order should prevent the dominance of any external power. China sees our Indo-Pacific initiatives as part of a U.S.-led policy of containing China. Russia's Foreign Ministry sees the Indo-Pacific as an American ploy to draw India and Japan into a military alliance against China and Russia. India's focus on economic links with the Russian Far East and activation of a Chennai-Vladivostok maritime corridor may help persuade Russia that its interests in the Pacific are compatible with our interest in diluting Chinese dominance in the Indo-Pacific; this also accords with President Putin's concept of a Greater Eurasia.

It needs to be noted that the RIC dynamics are sensitive to the configuration of the US-Russia-China triangle. This configuration changed in 2008 (the global economic crisis) and again in 2014 (Crimea's accession to Russia). COVID-19 has also triggered another painful change, which could be modulated by the outcome of the US Presidential elections, which may create an unexpected turmoil. The nature and impact of these changes, for now, is unknown.

As all the above factors impact the efficacy of the Triad, it may remain more of a show rather than an effective grouping, for at least a few more years to come, and any claims about its effectivity would sound hollow.

Analysis

It would be crystal clear that given the dimensions of the Indo-China relationship no meaningful outcome could be expected from the RIC dialogue. In view of this, India has to maintain a stable and meaningful relationship with Russia, to keep China's belligerence in check.

Russia's Emergence as "key mediator" in the China-India Imbroglio

As hopes for India-China rapprochement seem to be remote, at least in the immediate future, USA-Russia has been trying to find ways to diffuse the situation. However, China's belligerence has created hurdles in the path for any fruitful outcome.

Lukin (2020) in his study report on the subject has stated that—"The Indo-China relations were earlier hit by China's adventurism in Dokhlam. As if that wasn't enough May 2020, tensions along the disputed Sino-Indian border in Eastern Ladakh (a newly formed Indian union territory) spiralled dangerously out of control". It was because of unprovoked incursions by China in the Gulwan Valley and India's unprecedented reply to China.

US President Donald Trump offered to mediate, but neither New Delhi nor Beijing showed enthusiasm. Instead, Russia has become the *de facto* intermediary in the dispute, despite never publicly offering. Moscow's discreet diplomacy may have helped de-escalate the most violent China-India clash since the 1960s.

The conflict coincides with Russia's presidency of two key international forums: BRICS, a grouping of major non-Western powers Brazil, Russia, India, China and South Africa, and the Shanghai Cooperation Organisation (SCO). This presents Moscow with both a challenge and an opportunity.

The challenge is that India-China clash could derail BRICS and the SCO precisely when Moscow is chairing them. At the same time, Russia's chairing of the two institutions gives it the extra capacity to conduct pacifying diplomacy with New Delhi and Beijing and, in the process, raise its stature on the international stage. So far it seems the Kremlin has expertly taken advantage of the opportunity.

Since June 2020, Russia has engaged in efforts—albeit mostly behind-the-scenes—to facilitate de-escalation. On 23 June, a trilateral tele-meeting took place between the Russian, Indian and Chinese foreign ministers, presided over by Russian chief diplomat Sergey Lavrov. The conference's official agenda did not include the border standoff, but it was an achievement that Russia managed to bring together the Chinese and Indian foreign ministers amid continuing military tensions.

Lukin (2020) further pointed out that "The next visible step in this Russia-led trilateral diplomacy occurred in early September on the side-lines of SCO-related meetings in Moscow. The defence ministers of India and China had their first face-to-face meeting since the beginning of the crisis, followed a few days later by the first face-to-face talks between foreign ministers S Jaishankar and Wang Yi. The foreign ministers' meeting resulted in a joint statement listing five points of concurrence reached after a 'frank and constructive' discussion."

It is important to note how has Russia been able to achieve modest success, in defusing the crisis? For one thing, it helps that Moscow is on good terms with both sides, maintaining close 'strategic partnership' relations with both Beijing and New Delhi. And while Washington was quick to brand China the 'aggressor' in the Himalayan standoff, Moscow has carefully maintained neutrality and equidistance with respect to the dispute.

Russia also wields some leverage in its role as an important arms supplier, especially to India. In the wake of the flare-up in the Himalayas, Moscow agreed to New Delhi's requests to expedite deliveries on a previously concluded contract for the S-400 air defence system and to accelerate contract negotiations for the delivery of MiG-29 and Su-30 fighter jets. Granting India access to these advanced weapons is a stabilising move that preserves Russian credibility and makes India more confident.

The above view has been corroborated by Malhotra (2020) by pointing out that "The short point is Delhi needs Russia, not just because it has a credible epidemiological history and can offer a vaccine which may help India turn the corner, but because the Russians are the only big power today with cachet in Beijing, and can urge them to talk to Delhi on the Ladakh crisis.

She has rightly opined that "As Delhi seems to be once again walking down the road to Moscow. Much has changed, including the road itself, and there are many lessons to be relearnt—beginning from the fact that a foreign power's respect for you is directly proportional to your own strength."

Analysis

It is evident that India would need a strong ally like Russia to counter China as well as protect its national interests. India, therefore, should have no doubts about the importance of nurturing and deepening its relations with its time tested friend Russia.

Brief Evaluation of India's closeness to USA and QUAD/JAI Countries and Its Impact on Indo-Sino-Russia Relations

An analysis of the engaging feature of the current global situation would show the rise of China and the transformation of the Sino-Russian relationship from enmity to détente and now entente. In a considerable measure the relationship has been shaped by their estrangement with the West in general and the United States in particular.

Analysis of the Sino-Russian relationship would reveal that as Russian enmity with China had global consequences, so would their close friendship today. Both scenarios would have a serious impact on India, the former historically, and the latter in prospect. Russia has been a long-time friend of India, it not only provides India with sophisticated weapons, to maintain a formidable military profile, but also provided invaluable political support to India on a variety of regional/global issues. On the hand Transfer of military technology has been an important part of both the old and the new Russian-Chinese relationship, which has bothered India time and again. Another important factor for the greater depth of Sino-Russian relations relates to their growing economic ties based on cross border trade and Chinese investments in Russia, an area where India woefully lacks (Joshi 2019). These are the factors which India needs to ponder upon and put remedial measures in place.

India rightly does not, and should not, see this as a zero-sum game and has sought to engage both China and Russia bilaterally, as well as through a raft of organisations such as the Russia-India-China (RIC) grouping, the Shanghai Cooperation Organisation (SCO) and the Brazil, Russia, India China and South Africa (BRICS) grouping. But the given the uncertain nature of Chinese leadership, India more often than not has to be reactive in its approach towards China. Not surprisingly, given the relative imbalance of power between them, Russia often sees India as a means of balancing China. The Indo-Russia ties have their ups and downs attributable to the pressures on India due to its geographical location and geopolitical dynamics.

It needs to be noted that the current Sino-Russia ties stand on the Russia-Europe and China-US estrangement. But things can change, as they have in the past 60 years. Russia and China have been friends at one time enemies at another, likewise, the US/Europe and Russia. India is the only one that has remained largely with the same perspective that it had in the 1950s. Though the US has listed Russia as being at par with China as its strategic competitor, the reality is that only

China is competing and it is in US interests to keep Russia and China apart where India fits in. *Thus it's a complex game which is forcing Russia closer to China at the cost of India. India is thus forced to do a tight rope walk on the foreign relations front.*

To site an example, an engaging feature of India participating in the RIC at the side-lines of the G-20 in Buenos Aires in 2018 was that it also joined the leaders of Japan, the US is now called the JAI (Japan-America-India) trilateral. This was repeated at the June 2019 G 20 summit at Osaka where the Indian Prime Minister participated in both the RIC and the JAI summits as well (Joshi 2019).

By participating simultaneously in the JAI, Quad, RIC, the SCO and BRICS, India is signalling that it has its own views of these groupings and the Indo-Pacific concept. And in essence, its policy is pursuing the idea that a multipolar world is the one that suits its interests best.

Though India has a legitimate right to protect its interests, it also needs to appreciate that its QUAD and JAI ties would have an impact on its ties with China and Russia as well as China-Russia bilateral ties, even to the extent of binding China-Russia together strongly.

Analysis

It would be clear from the above that India today stands in an unenviable position. It cannot afford to annoy anyone—Russia, QUAD Countries or ASEAN if it has to have a strong counter China and also protect its interest in the Indo-Pacific Region, a tight rope walk indeed.

Specific Impact of QUAD on Indo-China-Russia Relations

Quad—Strengthening the Security Measures for India

Image Courtesy Wikimedia

India's participation and its roles in the Quadrilateral initiative with the United States, Japan, and Australia are now clear to China and Russia. This initiative that aims to combine capabilities and intent for a "free, open, prosperous and inclusive 'Indo-Pacific Region' has by and large been seen as a deterrent to China's rise in the region.

In addition, the emergence of the Indo-Pacific narrative has been seen by China and Russia as a probable threat to their interests. Tourangbam (2018) has pointed out that "This gigantic region has been the traditional theatre of Great Power politics and is also an area where China has been making strategic inroads. China's ambitious BRI covers both the maritime and continental pathways into Eurasia and has given more urgency to India's need to recalibrate its approach to the practice of strategic autonomy."

He opined that these mega-regions are entwined with India's economic and security interests. India must be nimble-footed in balancing its roles and responsibilities and executing an 'India first' foreign policy—one which takes full advantage of both bilateral and multilateral arrangements in the multipolar world order.

China-Russia Dissention of India's Engagements

Both China and Russia have openly expressed their displeasure about India's initiative related to QUAD.

Lee (2020) has pointed out that China feels that with QUAD "A direct countering of Beijing's 'win-win' BRI narrative—exposing the economic and political risks and costs of accepting Chinese funds—has already begun, but more can be done to shape the standards for conducting BRI projects and provide a practical and genuinely alternative source of infrastructure funding."

She opined that It is evident that from a strategic perspective China deciphers the primary value of the Quad *as a signal to Beijing* stating that the four states share a common intent to counter and thereby deter China from any further actions for changing the Indo-Pacific scenario. In view of the above, China has already started showing its disquiet about QUAD and has been trying to bring in Russia, to closely cooperate with it in containing the QUAD.

Not surprisingly, Russia has also openly said that it has conveyed to India on multiple occasions its concerns over the US-backed Quadrilateral coalition for the Indo-Pacific and held that introduction of competitive structures will create friction among the countries of the region.

In a press briefing (covered by Outlook 2020) Russian Ambassador Nikolai Kudashev said that "Moscow was concerned and apprehensive" over the Indo-Pacific strategy of the US as it has completely ignored the existence of Russia and

China while pushing forward its agenda for the strategically key region.

He went on to, say that "We need to deepen our mutual understanding of the events evolving in the Pacific Ocean and the Indian Ocean ... Why should we introduce some competitive structure to divide the countries of the region rather than bringing them together," the Russian envoy said.

It's amply clear that both China and Russia are not very happy with India's closeness with the USA, its association with QUAD and JAI. Accordingly, there is a strong possibility that these circumstances might have propelled China and Russia in strengthening their relationship.

Analysis

In summary, it could be said that China-Russia may contemplate the conclusion of a *"Military Pact"* as a counter to the emerging Indo-Pacific scenario and not directly aimed against India. But no one would need an astrologer to predict its direct impact on India in Geo-Socio-Politico-Economic as well as Military and Strategic spheres. India cannot afford to be ignorant about this destabilising impact and urgency for putting remedial measures in place to minimise the consequences.

4. Assessment of Impact

Probable Impact of Sino-Russia Military Pact on India

Given the complex nature of the issues involved and the conflicting national interests of each country, it would not be easy to analyse the exact impact of the Sino-Russian Military Pact on India. What best can be done is to broad-brush a canvass.

On this topic Weigold (2019b) has said that "There are some basic questions which would need to be answered: We all know why India needs Russia. But just what place does India have in Russia's global strategy? Is it merely a hedge against the US and China or something more?"

He said that for reasons of its own, Historically India has always maintained its stance on maintaining its strategic autonomy and links with Russia and China. Russia is a special case here. Though India's formal trade with Russia may not be significant but it remains vital for India's defence posture. Leave alone the present, in the immediate future, India may have to seek Russian help to build nuclear attack submarines and hypersonic vehicles. This is because India feels that despite its close ties with the US, Washington is unlikely to provide them with such high-tech wherewithal. Not having such systems would seriously imbalance India's military capabilities in relation to China.

In addition, even though India does not share the US or Japanese concepts of the Free and Open Indo-Pacific (FOIP), it is a member of the Quadrilateral or Quad group comprising of the US, Australia, Japan and India which is aimed at countering China. Russia's understanding of India's compulsions would be a necessity.

All the above points, where India would expect Russia's support would be impacted by formal Sino-Russia Military Pact—which could be a big blow to India.

Compulsions of Russia and the Impact on Russia-India Equation

India would need to certainly understand Russia's compulsions for strengthening its relations with China. Indian defence News (IDN 2020) has outlined Russia's compulsions as follows:

- It has alternately been shunned, lured and targeted by the west, resulting in progressive loss of influence and a sense of siege. It was invited to join the prestigious G7 grouping in 1998 but was dropped in 2014. The last straw was the overtures of the European Union (EU) and NATO to Ukraine. Kiev has since become a 'priority partner' of the EU, and an 'Enhanced Opportunity Partner' of NATO. Upset, disillusioned and isolated, Russia made common cause with China, to shore up its flanks.
- Russia values India and China as important diplomatic partners and has been trying to push trilateral engagement. For example, India was reluctant to join the RIC (Russia, India and China) forum but Russia persuaded her.

Similarly, Russia actively supported India's membership of SCO (Shanghai Cooperation Organisation).

- Therefore, even though the Sino-Indian estrangement bothers Russia, but it is careful about not offering its good offices.
- Russia-China cohabitation is less a marriage of convenience and more an open live-in relationship, adaptable to evolving circumstances. But at this juncture China-Russia needs each other, thus weakening India's leverage with Russia.

Analysis

The complete narrative above could be summed in a single line "*No Denying That Russia-China Ties Do Impact Russia-India Equation*".

Possible Indian Strategy to Retain Russia in its Camp

India has to accept that some adverse effects of the 'Sino-Russia Pact' on India, in geo-politico economic and security spheres would be unavoidable. It would be, thus, imperative for India to do some out of the box thinking to ensure that Russia remains on its side and helps India in safeguarding its multi-dimensional interests. Some impotent measures could cover:

- Assuring Russia that India's growing ties with USA/ QUAD/JAI Countries will never be at the cost of the primacy of India's long-standing, time tested relationship with Russia.
- Remind Russia that it is India's principal defence partner. A significant percentage of India's arms imports in the last 5 years came from Russia. Both sides are now desirous of

moving away from buyer-seller relations and undertake joint development and production.

- Leverage India's good cooperation in the energy sector. India has already invested US$ 15 billion in the Russian hydrocarbon sector. Russia is the only country to build nuclear power plants in India.
- Remember that Russia's relationship with China rests on three shaky pillars:
    - Peaceful Boundary—Xi's talk of "rejuvenation of the Chinese Nation" has raised fears about Chinese revanchism, in Russia's mind.
    - Expanding Trade—As for the economic pillar, Russia realises that while Russia presently enjoys a nominal trade surplus, going beyond gross trade to value-added trade, China has a clear advantage going forward. Russia also remains wary about allowing any dominating role for China in the oil and gas sector.
    - Shared distrust of American intentions—As for their shared dislike of Washington, each still hopes to repair ties and, therefore, neither trusts the other fully with regard to the third pillar.
- Remind Russia that it cannot be oblivious to the fact that China is both a strategic competitor and friend. Even while deferring to Russia in the Central Asian connection, Beijing is building connectivity linkages to Europe that bypasses its current Russian connection. Its relationship to Central Asia is undermining the Russian influence in the region.
- Despite the above, India needs to ensure that greater and real impetus gets infused in the relationship which is proving to be difficult, as trade remains sluggish.

The author opines that India needs to explore the above-stated measures to gain maximum leverage and achieve its aim of containing China, without jeopardising its relationships with countries important for safeguarding its national interests. The author would also like to acknowledge valuable assistance received from an article by Gokhale (2020a).

Ghokhale (2020a) has cited a comment by Sumit Ganguly, who in his article on "Foreign Policy, made out a case for India to re-calculate its relationship with Russia". His contention has been that:

> The politically reliable, trustworthy defence supplier with shared misgivings about the Dragon, that was the Soviet Union of yore, has long been replaced by a politically agnostic, commercially motivated Russia that no longer shares our concerns about China. This might be valid if China is the *principal factor* in our relations with Russia, but that is not the case. It never was even in the 1960s and the 1970s. A strategic partnership with Russia based on the absence of fundamental conflicts of interest and a shared belief that some form of multi-polarity is better than any sort of Sino-U.S. condominium is important for India, and this relationship deserves more attention from both sides. In the words of Prime Minister Indira Gandhi in Moscow on September 20, 1982, "the garden of friendship like all gardens must be consistently tended".

Finally, no one could have summed it better than India's Hon. Minister for Foreign Affairs, Jaishankar (2020) said that "This is a time for us to engage America, *manage*

China, cultivate Europe, *reassure Russia*, bring Japan into play, draw neighbours in, extend the neighbourhood and expand traditional constituencies of support." He added that "Refreshing India's ties with Russia has required dedicated efforts." Those efforts need to be sustained and gains made consolidated.

Analysis

From the above analysis, it's clear that Sino-Russia strong ties would impact India in various spheres. But all is not lost. With concerted efforts, careful balancing of its relationships with the western world, and keeping Russia diplomatically informed that containing China is a compulsion for both India and Russia; India may still be able to do the proverbial tight rope walk.

5. Conclusion and Recommendations

India geographically stands in a difficult region where it has been practically isolated from its neighbours by China with its smart but nefarious designs. India has been facing issues with the Belt and Road Initiative of China, China's belligerence in the South China Sea, China's unabated provocations on the Indian borders, proxy provocations by China through Pakistan and Nepal and the list could go on....

Given the Sino-Russia relationship, it is quite apparent that Russia would not like to openly take sides in Indo-Sino disputes. Thus India has been almost forced to deepen its relationship with the USA and QUAD countries. Support of the USA and QUAD would be important for India to safeguard its geo-political-strategic-economic interests as well as its interests is emerging Indo-Pacific region.

On the other hand, India's deepening relationships with the USA and QUAD have also not been taken kindly by both China and Russia—formal feeling threatened and later feeling betrayed. This has pushed China-Russia in a tighter embrace, a fact which is becoming unpalatable for USA-QUAD counties and India.

It is, therefore, important to synthesise India's situation, which may look like as follows:

- Containment of China would be the top priority for India.
- To achieve the above India would need to deepen its relationships with the USA and QUAD counties.

- While doing that India would need to reassure Russia that its other relationships would never be at the cost of time tested Indo-Russia relationship.

Thus a tight rope walk is inevitable for India for maintaining its relationships with various countries. Following suggestions are made:

- Global Isolations of China—Currently China is on a sticky wicket with ASEAN, Australia, Japan, Myanmar, Sri Lanka either because of China's belligerence in the South China Sea, debt trap sprung by China on many countries or China's apparent mishandling of COVID-19 crisis. India needs to use this situation to its fullest advantage by building a global consensus against China thus isolating it diplomatically.
- Develop its geo-politico-socio-cultural-defence relationships with ASEAN and BIMSTC countries and create an effective 'Soft Border' between China and India.
- India should offer developmental, financial (maybe through mechanisms like lines of credit) and Defence (Security) support to ASEAN and BIMSTEC Countries, to build interdependent relationships.
- Deepen relationships with Russia in Trade, Cultural, Social, Educational, Energy, Defence spheres thus reassuring Russia of the primacy of its relationship for India. Encourage more manufacturing partnerships under Make in India. through Technology Transfer from Russia.
- Nurture its relationships with the USA, QUAD Countries to build an effective deterrence to contain China at its

borders and in IOR/South China Sea/Indo-Pacific Region.

- Build consistency in its relationships with other countries.
- Last but not the least, reduce internal strife, build political consensus. improve decision making efficiency and do not allow state politics to impinge upon Foreign Relationships.

Finally, the author would like to say that numerous constraints being currently faced by India are well understood. However, when the situation comes to matters of national security and national wellbeing, Government needs to take some tough decisions, banking on the maturity of the nation's citizens, who have always stood with the government and risen to the occasion during times of crisis.

Though the author has tried to do justice to the topic as much as feasible, it is not possible to cover all the aspects. Thus a few issues, which would need further research, cover:

- Impact of probable change of guard in USA on USA-China-Russia relationship, Indo-US relationship, QUAD's strength, the situation on which is still not clear.
- Impact of counter QUAD (Pakistan-Iran-Turkey, Malaysia) will have on the Indo-China-Russia relationship.
- Impact of India being drawn into a war-like situation by China on Indo-Russia and Indo-US Relationships and India's tottering economy.
- Constraints faced by India due to internal strife and political wrangles.

References

Aliyev, Nurlan, July 1, 2020, "RKKK-ICDS, Military Cooperation between Russia and China: The Military Alliance without an Agreement?", Retrieved from https://icds.ee/en/military-cooperation-between-russia-and-china-themilitary-alliance-without-an-agreement/, accessed on November 2, 2020.

Belt and Road News, November 30, 2019, beltandroad.news Retrieved from: www.belrandroad,news/2019/11/30/chinas-belt-road-resume-ancient-traderoutes-as-silk-roads/, accessed on October 12, 2020.

Bhattacharya Abanti, April 2004(a&b), "The Fallacy in the Russia-India-China Triangle", Strategic Analysis Vol 28, Issue 2, Retrieved from https://idsa.in/strategicanalysis/TheFallacyintheRussiaIndiaChinaTriangle_abhattacharya_0404, accessed on October 24-25, 2020.

Bhattacharya, Abanti, Apr 2004, "The Fallacy in the Russia-India-China Triangle", Strategic Analysis Vol 28, Issue 2, Retrieved from https://idsa.in/strategicanalysis/TheFallacyintheRussiaIndiaChinaTriangle_abhattacharya_0404, accessed on October 24-25. 2020.

Bhattacharya, Abanti, April 2004(b), "The Fallacy in the Russia-India-China Triangle", Strategic Analysis, Vol 28, Issue 2, Retrieved from https://idsa.in/strategicanalysis/TheFallacyintheRussiaIndiaChinaTriangle_abhattacharya_0404, accessed on October 24-25, 2020.

Bowen, Andrew S., August 20, 2020, "Russian Armed Forces: Military Doctrine and Strategy", Congressional Research Service (CRS), Retrieved from https://fas.org/sgp/crs/row/IF11625.pdf, accessed on October 25-28, 2020.

Chaudhary, Smriti, October 30, 2020, "Crack Appearing In Pakistan, China Relations As Beijing Demands Higher Interest Under CPEC?", Eurasiatimes, Retrieved from https://eurasiantimes.com/crack-appearing-in-pakistanchina-relations-as-beijing-demands-higher-interest-under-cpec/, accessed on November 1, 2020.

Chinoy, SR, January 13, 2021, "A history fact-check for China" Indian Express (Print Edition), accessed on January 13, 2021.

Clay, William, Quote, Retrieved from https://www.forbes.com/quotes/9781/, accessed on October 24, 2020.

Cordesman, Anthony H (Arleigh A. Burke Chair in Strategy), July 24, 2019, China's New 2019 Defense White Paper, Center for Strategic and International Studies, Retrieved from https://www.csis.org/analysis/chinas-new-2019-defensewhite-paper, accessed on October 24-27-29, 2029.

Dey, Aninda, October 1, 2020-2020a. Times of India Blog (Make it Count). Return of the dragon: US boots won't land in Ladakh, Retrieved from https://timesofindia.indiatimes.com/blogs/words-worth/return-of-the-dragon-usboots-wont-land-in-ladakh/, accessed on October 28-29 and November 2, 2020.

Georgy Zhukov, Quote, Retrieved from: http://www.morefamousquotes.com/authors/georgy-zhukov-quotes/, accesed on October 27, 2020.

Gokhale, Vijay, August 20, 2020, "China-Russia ties as a major determinant", The Hindu, Retrieved from https://www.thehindu.com/opinion/lead/chinarussia-ties-as-a-major-determinant/article32397585.ece, accessed on October 24-25-November 1, 2020.

Gokhale, Vijay, August 20, 2020, "China-Russia ties as a major determinant", The Hindu, Retrieved from https://www.thehindu.com/opinion/lead/chinarussia-ties-as-a-major-determinant/article32397585.ece, accessed on October 24-25-November 1, 2020.

Indian Defence News, September 9, 2020, "India-China Clash: Why Russia Won't Mediate but will Ease Tension", Retrieved from http://www.indiandefensenews.in/2020/09/india-china-clash-why-russia-wont.html, accessed on October 29-November 2, 2020.

Jaishankar, S., September 13, 2020, "India needs a refined tool kit to manage China", Hindustan Times, Retrieved from https://www.pressreader.com/, accessed on October 24-25-November 2, 2020.

Joshi, Manoj, December 20 , 2019(a), "India's strategy in the China-RussiaUSA triangle", Observer Research Foundation, Retrieved from https://www.orfonline.org/research/indias-strategy-in-the-china-russia-usatriangle-59417/, accessed on October 26-27 and November 1, 2020.

Joshi, Manoj, December 20, 2019(a), "India's strategy in the China-RussiaUSA triangle", Observer Research Foundation, Retrieved from https://www.orfonline.org/research/indias-strategy-in-the-china-russia-usatriangle-59417/, accessed on October 26-27 and November 1, 2020.

Kuczy ski, Grzegorz, May 18, 2020, "Russia-China: a limited liability military alliance", The Kuczy ski, Grzegorz, May 18, 2020a, "Russia-China: a limited liability military alliance", The Warsaw Institute Review, Retrieved from https://warsawinstitute.review/issue-2020/russia-china-a-limited-liability-military-alliance/, accessed on October 25-29, 2020.

Kuczy ski, Grzegorz, May 18, 2020a, "Russia-China: a limited liability military alliance", The Warsaw Institute Review, Retrieved from https://warsawinstitute.review/issue-2020/russia-china-a-limited-liability-military-alliance/, accessed on October 25-29, 2020. Warsaw Institute Review, Retrieved from https://warsawinstitute.review/issue-2020/russia-china-a-limited-liability-military-alliance/, accessed on October 25-29, 2020.

Lee, Lavina, May 19, 2020, "Assessing the QUAD: Prospects and Limitations of Quadrilateral Cooperation for Advancing Australia's Interests", Lowyn Institute, Retrieved from https://www.lowyinstitute.org/PUBLICATIONS/ASSESSING-QUAD-PROSPECTS-AND-LIMITATIONSQUADRILATERAL-COOPERATION-ADVANCING-AUSTRALIA, accessed on October 31-November 1 and 2, 2020.

Lintner, Bertil, October 30, 2020, "Behind China's threat to support insurgency in India", Asia Times, Retrieved from https://asiatimes.com/2020/10/behindchinas-threat-to-support-insurgency-in-india/, accessed on November 1, 2020.

Lukin, Artyom, October 23, 2020, "How Russia emerged as key mediator in the China-India dispute", East Asia Forum, Retrieved from https://www.eastasiaforum.org/2020/10/23/how-russia-emerged-as-key-mediator-inthe-china-india-dispute/, accessed on October 25-26 and November 2, 2020.

Malhotra, Jyoti, September 8, 2020, "Russia makes a comeback into India's plans: All thanks to China and Covid", The Print, Retrieved from https://theprint.in/opinion/global-print/russia-makes-a-comeback-into-indias-plans-all-thankssto-china-and-covid/497977/, accessed on October 27-28 and November 2, 2020.

Massicot, Dara, September 9, 2019(a&b), "Anticipating A New Russian Military Doctrine in 2020: What It Might Contain And Why It Matters", War On The Rocks, Retrieved from https://warontherocks.com/2019/09/anticipatinga-new-russian-military-doctrine-in-2020-what-it-might-contain-and-why-itmatters/, accessed on October 25-29, 2020.

Massicot, Dara, September 9, 2019, "Anticipating A New Russian Military Doctrine in 2020: What It Might Contain And Why It Matters", War On The Rocks, Retrieved from https://warontherocks.com/2019/09/anticipating-a-newrussian-military-doctrine-in-2020-what-it-might-contain-and-why-it-matters/, accessed on October 25-29, 2020.

Military Strategy-Definition, Encyclopaedia Britannica, Retrieved from https://www.britannica.com/topic/strategy-military, accessed on October 30, 2020.

Ministry of External Affairs, Government of India (MEA GOI), August 7, 1971, "Treaty of Peace, Friendship and Co-operation *Russia". Retrieved from https://mea.gov.in/bilateral-documents.htm?dtl/5139/Treaty+of+, accessed on October 24-25, 2020.

Muni, SD, March 2016, "India and China Relations: Historical, cultural and Security Issues", (Foreword) (By Reddy JG), Researchgate, Retrieved from: https://www.researchgate.net/publication/301294515_India_and_China_Relations_Historical_cultural_and_Security_Issues, accessed on October 30, 2020.

Nixon, Richard M, Quote, Retrieved from https://quotefancy.com/quote/1345587/Richard-M-Nixon-A-riot-is-a-spontaneous-outburst-A-war-is-subject-to-advance-planning, accessed on October 29, 2020.

Nouwens, Meia, July 26, 2019, "China's 2019 Defence White Paper: Report Card on Military Reform", IISS, Retrieved from https://www.iiss.org/blogs/analysis/2019/07/china-2019-defence-white-paper, accessed on October 24, 2020.

Nouwens, Meia, July 26, 2019a, "China's 2019 Defence White Paper: Report Card on Military Reform", IISS, Retrieved from https://www.iiss.org/blogs/analysis/2019/07/china-2019-defence-white-paper, accessed on October 24 to 27, 2020.

Nouwens, Meia, July 26, 2019a, "China's 2019 Defence White Paper: Report Card on Military Reform", IISS, Retrieved from https://www.iiss.org/blogs/analysis/2019/07/china-2019-defence-white-paper, accessed on October 24, 2020.

O'Rourke, Ronald, August 5, 2020, "Congressional Research Service Report 2020", U.S. Role in the World: Background & Issues for Congress R44891, Retrieved from https://www.andrewerickson.com/2020/08/updated-crsreport-offers-major-china-russia-coverage-u-s-role-in-the-world-backgroundissues-for-congress/, accessed on October 28, 2020 and January 13, 2021.

Outlook (The News Scroll), January 17, 2020, "Conveyed our concerns to India on ''Quad'' on multiple occasions: Russian Ambassador", Retrieved from https://www.outlookindia.com/newsscroll/conveyed-our-concerns-to-india-on-quadon-multiple-occasions-russian-ambassador/1711096, accessed on October 29-30, 2020.

Pant, Harsh V., October 29, 2020, "Beijing's aggression has made India's diffidence about alignment obsolete", India Defence News, Retrieved from http://www.indiandefensenews.in/2020/10/beijings-aggression-has-made-indias.html, accessed on November 2, 2020.

Putin, Vladimir-Quote, October 22, 2020, The Times of India, Retrieved from https://timesofindia.indiatimes.com/world/europe/putin-russia-chinamilitary-alliance-cant-be-ruled-out/articleshow/78816186.cms

Raghavan, PS, July 29, 2020, "RIC, a triangle that is still important", The Hindu, Retrieved from https://www.thehindu.com/opinion/lead/ric-a-trianglethat-is-still-important/article32215791.ece, accessed on October 25-26 and November 1, 2020.

Rajagopalan, Rajesh, June 18, 2020, "India can't free-ride others to limit China. It needs to lead the containment strategy", The Print, Retrieved from https://theprint.in/opinion/india-cant-free-ride-others-to-limit-china-it-needs-tolead-the-containment-strategy/443687/, accessed on November 1, 2020.

Reddy, Jayachandra Gundre, March 2016, "India and China Relations: Historical, cultural and Security Issues", Researchgate, Retrieved from https://www.researchgate.net/publication/301294515_India_and_China_Relations_Probable Sino-Russia Military Pact-Implications for India Historical_cultural_and_Security_Issues, accessed on October 24-25-30, 2020.

Report to Congress on Russian Military Doctrine and Strategy. August 21, 2020, Retrieved from https://news.usni.org/2020/08/21/report-to-congresson-russian-military-doctrine-and-strategy, accessed on October 28, 2020 and January 13, 2021.

Roosevelt, Franklin D, Quote, Retrieved from https://www.pinterest.com/twinndes/fdr-quotes/, accessed on October 24, 2020.

Sardzhyan, Simon and Flood, Angelina (Quotes Zwack Peter), June 14, 2019, Russia Matters-BelferCenter for Science and International Affairs (Harvard Kennedy School), Expert Round-Up: How Likely Is a China-Russia Military Alliance? Retrieved from https://www.russiamatters.org/analysis/expert-round-howlikely-china-russia-military-alliance, accessed on October 24-25, 2020.

Sun, Tzu, Quote, Retrieved from https://www.google.com/search?q=wikimedia+photo+of+sun+tzu+quotes&tbm=isch&chips=q:wikimedia+photo+of+sun+tzu+quotes,online_chips:strategy&rlz=1C1RXQR_enIN931IN931&hl, accessed on January 13, 2021.

The Warsaw Institute, May 18, 2020, "Russia-China: a limited liability military alliance", The Warsaw Institute Review, Retrieved from https://warsawinstitute.review/issue-2020/russia-china-a-limited-liability-military-alliance/, accessed on October 24-25 and November 1, 2020.

The Warsaw Institute, May 18, 2020, "Russia-China: a limited liability military alliance", The Warsaw Institute Review, Retrieved from https://warsawinstitute.review/issue-2020/russia-china-a-limited-liability-military-alliance/, accessed on October 24-25 and November 1, 2020.

Tourangbam, Monish, July 24, 2018, "Asia and Pacific Policy Society, India's Balancing Act", Policy Forum, Retrieved from https://www.policyforum.net/indias-balancing-act/, accessed on October 31 and November 1, 2020.

USNI News, 26 May 2015, Document: China's Military Strategy, USNI News, Retrieved from https://news.usni.org/2015/05/26/document-chinasmilitary-strategy, accessed on October 23-24-31, 2020.

Warsaw Institute Special Report, "Chinese-Russian Unequal Partnership", Warsaw Institute, 27.06.2019 (Daniel Coats Quote), Retrieved from https://warsawinstitute.org/chinese-russian-unequal-partnership/ accessed on October 30-31, 2020.

Weigold, Auriol Dr, July 9, 2020(a), "Future Direction International, India and Russia: An Unbroken, Long-Term Relationship", Retrieved from https://www.futuredirections.org.au/publication/india-and-russia-an-unbroken-longterm-relationship/, accessed on October 25-26-30, 2020.

Weigold, Auriol Dr, July 9, 2020(a), "Future Direction International, India and Russia: An Unbroken, Long-Term Relationship", Retrieved from https://www.futuredirections.org.au/publication/india-and-russia-an-unbroken-longterm-relationship/, accessed on October 25-26-30, 2020

Postscript

Almost nine months have gone past since writing this monograph. Meanwhile, the scenario has changed drastically, necessitating addition of this postscript. Some major events which have enhanced the 'probability of China-Russia Military Pact' are:

a. USA's withdrawal from Afghanistan and related issues
b. Signing of AUKUS Security Accord
c. Events indicating strengthening of QUAD

The US withdrawal from Afghanistan and China-Russia Common Interests

With the Taliban back in charge in Afghanistan, post United States withdrawal, attention has turned to the United States' main competitors: China and Russia. Moscow and Beijing are likely to experience both a convergence and clash of interests when it comes to Afghanistan, but their long experience in dividing up influence in Central Asia offers a likely path forward (Chausovasky, 2021). The US failure and messy withdrawal are quite significant in China's playbook. China perceives failure of United States as an opportunity for demonstrating its own agnostic approach to political systems and governance. China would consider its own model of building peace through economic development. In Beijing's view, success in rebuilding and stabilising Afghanistan could allow China to prove to world its superiority over the United States—as a global leader. However, China's concerns about Uyghurs in China and safety of China Pakistan Economic Corridor and likely upsurge of terrorism in the region may compel it to be militarily prepared to safeguard its own interests.

On the other hand, Russia would look for preventing the spread of instability from Afghanistan to bordering Central Asian states, terrorist attacks against Russia from groups based in Afghanistan, and support for radicalism in Russia. Russia would also like to see a reduction in drug trafficking headed north, but this is a tertiary goal. Thus both China and Russia have their own interests to protect and adaption a collaborative approach by them cannot be ruled out (Kofman et al., 2021).

Australia-United Kingdom-US (AUKUS) Security Accord

The Aukus defence pact between the US, UK and Australia may drive China to step up its efforts to enhance its anti-submarine capabilities, military analysts have said. The three-nation alliance will give Australia access to nuclear-powered submarine technology and is seen as a way of increasing the pressure on China in the Asia-Pacific (Wong, 2021).

Russia also has commented on AUKUS, stating that the AUKUS defense partnership (Australia, the UK and the US) is aimed against China. "The initiative causes very serious questions," said Russian Permanent Representative to international organisations in Vienna Mikhail Ulyanov. The Russian envoy also noted that this is the first initiative announced by the three countries, which means that it will be followed by second and third ones (TASS, 2021). In addition to the above, Russian Security Council Secretary Nikolai Patrushev described the AUKUS alliance of Australia, the United Kingdom and the United States as another military bloc directed against Russia and China, also emphasizing that this "venture" puts the entire Asian security architecture at risk (Sputnik, 2021).

QUAD Summit in Washington

Ahead of the first in-person QUAD summit among the leaders of the US, India, Japan and Australia in Washington (25 September 2021), China on criticised the grouping, saying the formation of exclusive closed cliques runs against the trend of times, and it is doomed to fail. Chinese Foreign Ministry spokesman Zhao Lijian told the media that the quadrilateral grouping should not target any third country and its interests (PTI, 2021). Further, Russia's objections to the QUAD have been well known. Addressing the media in reference to QUAD, the Russian Ambassador to India Nikolai Kudashev had said Moscow was "concerned and apprehensive" over the Indo-Pacific strategy of the US as it had completely ignored the existence of Russia and China while pushing forward its agenda for the strategically important region (Times Now Digital, 2020). Analysts have opined that QUAD has spurred the acceleration in Sino-Russian defense cooperation. The above observation is in line with the reported discussions during foreign ministers meeting in response to the QUAD, where in Russian foreign minister Sergey Lavrov was highly critical of the quadrilateral format and signalled the coordination of Russia-China policy positions and the strengthening of relations. Indicators are already there that as the United States and its allies are increasing their strategic posture in the Indo-Pacific, Russia's defense cooperation with Beijing would grow. This is because it's China—than any other Asian power-which can help Russia enhance its standing globally, and in the Indo-Pacific region to a lesser extent. Moscow is expected to subordinate its relations with other regional powers, such as India and Vietnam, to its strategic partnership with Beijing (Conley et al., 2021).

Summary

All the above events have a strong potential to enhance the 'Possibility of Sino-Russia Military Pact'.

It would also impact India complicating its geo-politico-strategic-economic-military situation. Keeping these foreseen impacts in mind India needs to undertake holistic review of the prevailing situation and recalibrate its strategy for safeguarding its own national interests.

References

Chausovasky Eugene (September 13, 2021), China and Russia Have a Shared Playbook for Afghanistan, Foreign Policy, In Line, Retrieved From: https://foreignpolicy.com/2021/09/13/china-russia-shared-playbook-afghanistan/, Accessed on September 29, 2021.

Kofman Michael, AARON Stein Aaron, Sun Yun (August 31, 2021) AFTER WITHDRAWAL: HOW CHINA, TURKEY, AND RUSSIA WILL RESPOND TO THE TALIBAN, War On Rocks, On Line, Retrieved From: https://warontherocks.com/2021/08/after-withdrawal-how-china-turkey-and-russia-will-respond-to-the-taliban/, Accessed on September 29, 2021.

Wong Catherine (September 25, 2021), Aukus security pact likely to spur China into boosting anti-submarine warfare capacity, SCMP, On Line, Retrieved From: https://www.scmp.com/news/china/diplomacy/article/3150118/aukus-security-pact-likely-spur-china-boosting-anti-submarine, Accessed on September 29, 2021.

TASS (September 27, 2021), AUKUS partnership aimed against China, Russian envoy to Vienna says, TASS, On Line, Retrieved From: https://tass.com/world/1339103, Accessed on September 29, 2021.

Sputnik (September 21, 2021), After NATO & QUAD, Russian Security Council Chief Says New Block – AUKUS – Directed Against Russia, China, The Eurasian Times, On Line, Retrieved From: https://eurasiantimes.com/after-nato-quad-russian-security-council-chief-says-new-block-aukus-directed-against-russia-china/, Accessed on September 29, 2021.

PTI Beijing (September 24, 2021), China slams Quad ahead of 1st in-person summit in US, says doomed to fail', Business Standard On Line, Retrieved From: https://www.business-standard.com/article/international/china-slams-quad-ahead-of-1st-in-person-summit-in-us-says-doomed-to-fail-121092401203_1.html, Accessed on September 29, 2021.

Times Now Digital (January 17, 2020), After calling 'Quad' divisive, Russia says India will not deny anybody opportunity in Pacific, Times Now Digital, On Line, Retrieved From: https://www.timesnownews.com/india/article/after-calling-quad-divisive-russia-says-india-will-not-deny-anybody-opportunity-in-pacific/541622#:~:text=After%20calling%20%E2%80%98Quad%E2%80%99%20divisive%2C%20Russian%20Ambassador%20Nikolai%20Kudashev,Russian%20President%20Vladimir%20Putin%20%7C%20Photo%20Credit%3A%20IANS, Accessed on September 29, 2021.

Conley Heather A, Green Michael J, Szechenyi Nicholas, Newlin Cyrus (April 06, 2021), The Return of the Quad: Will Russia and China Form Their Own Bloc?, Center for Strategic and International studies (CSIS), On Line, Retrieved From: https://www.csis.org/analysis/return-quad-will-russia-and-china-form-their-own-bloc, Accessed on September 29, 2021.

About the Author

Commodore SL Deshmukh, Nausena Medal (Retired), has served in the Indian Navy for 32 years. His educational qualifications include BE (Mech), MSc (Def Sc), PGDM (Gold Medallist). He holds a qualification both in Marine & Aviation fields. He served on-board ships & Aircraft carriers. He is a specialist in the maintenance of Fighter aircraft and Anti Submarines Warfare Helicopters. He held many operational and administrative appointments including Principal Director at Naval HQ, Commodore Superintendent Naval Aircraft Yard, Director Naval Institute of Aeronautical Technology and Project Director of a major Naval Aviation Project. He is alumni of Defence Services Staff College (Wellington, Nilgiris).

Post-retirement from Indian Navy he worked with Tata Group for 5 years and is currently working with SUN Group's Aerospace & Defence vertical (at Gurgaon) as Senior Vice President. He has presented papers at various International Seminars and has many other research papers to his credit. He is a Life Member of Aeronautical Society of India.

He also works in the educational field in his spare time. He is an avid writer and navigates through poetry at one end and matter related to technology and defence as well as issues of common interest.

CPSIA information can be obtained
at www.ICGtesting.com
Printed in the USA
LVHW032123240323
742526LV00007B/473

9 789391 490287